There's something you should know.
Truth be told, you already know it.
You just don't know you know it, but we'll remind you now.
We'll draw it down, like the moon, to the front of your brain,
in that dark space just behind your eyes—
that space that goes all the way down your throat and into your gullet.
Close your eyes and take a breath. Fill that space.
Count to three, then open your eyes and read the next words.
Whenever you're ready.
We'll wait...

Now.
Here we are.
All of us Witches.
We are in everything. Every story. Every century.
Every society. Every last corner of the planet.
Even if they call us by other names, we are what we are.
The gravest mistake is to think we have slipped into myth, fallen into legend—
to think we aren't still moving through your mirrors, or waiting in the tangled woods.
To think that we have forgotten what was done to us—
that we haven't hexed your homes, or that we won't curse your children.
To think that, someday, we won't eat your children.

To think that, someday, we won't claw our way up and through you—
out of your gaping mouth, eating you, twisting ourselves backwards as we bite.
Do you see it now?
Do you recognize us?
We are always here. You dream us, you fear us, you honor us.
And the way we know you know us is because for every time you've howled in pain,
for every time you've laughed and screamed at the sky,
for every time you spoke to an animal and knew they understood,
for every time the animal spoke back...
for every time you've felt ancient, transient, and powerful,
and for every time you heard the call of the void and felt nothing...
for every single story you ever weave, for every lie,
for every truth, for every curse, and every healing spell,
for every lucky guess, and for all the times you know...
The Witch in you wakes up.
Look in the mirror and see.
We are here.

- Donna Lynch   December 2017

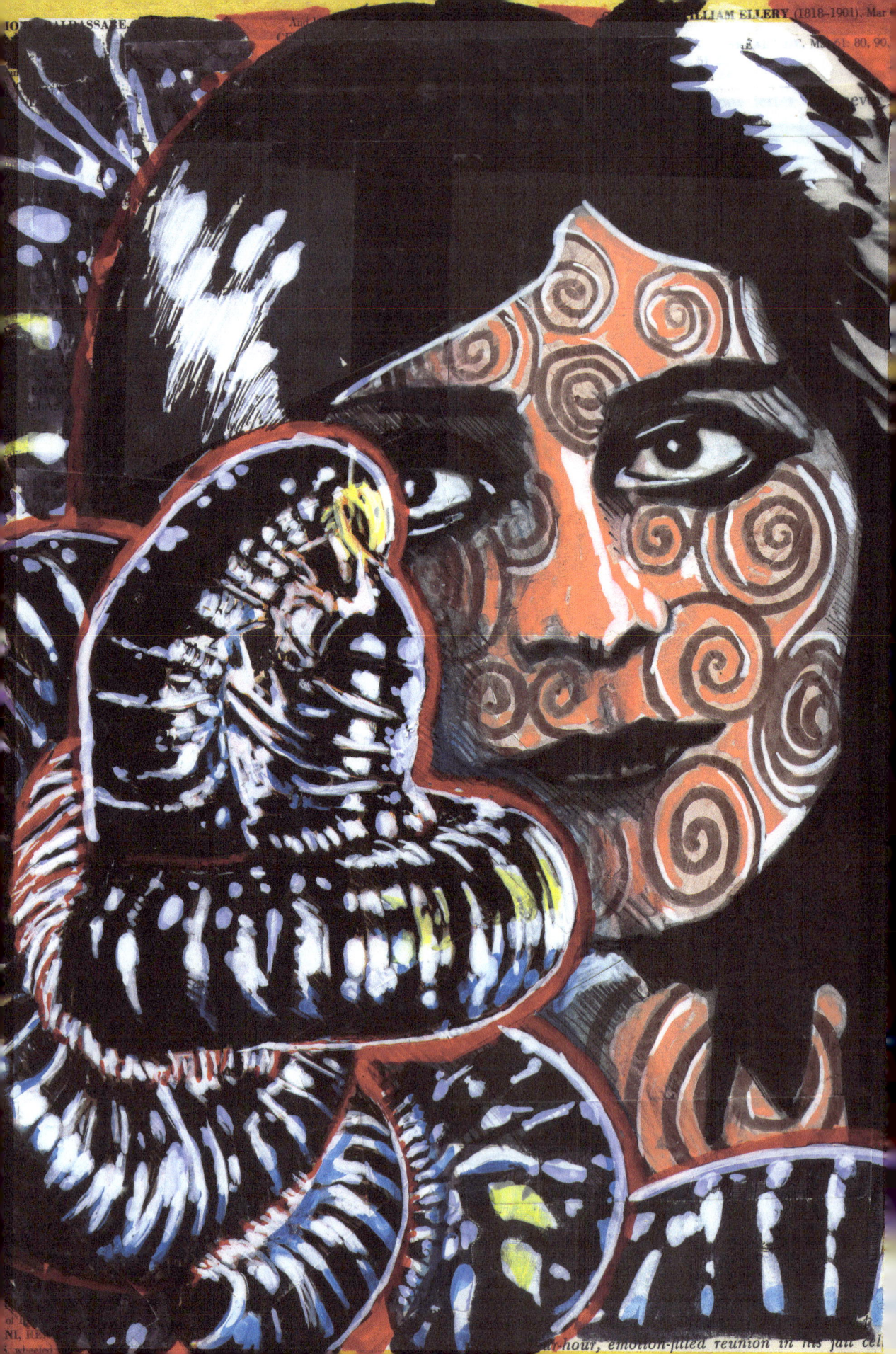

The Bruja of the Winding Path

The first bite the Devil took

gave her magic.

The second gave her wisdom.

The third, intuition.

After that they were just for kicks.

But mind you, little ones,

because she bites, too.

For different reasons.

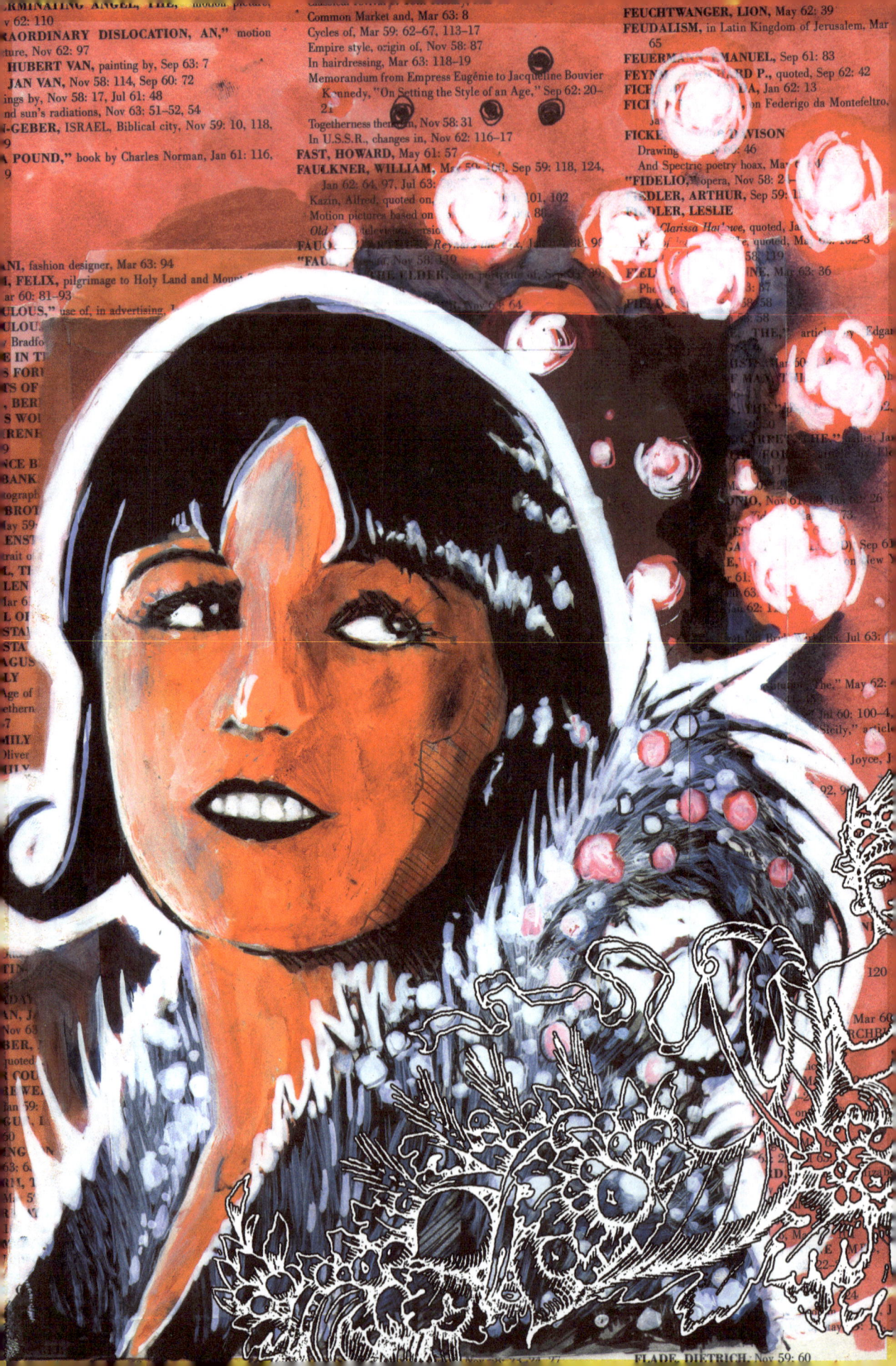

Morgan Le Fay and the Algonquin Round Table

She ensnared you in charms and a coy, crooked smile

With her eyes like the stars and her feminine wiles

She laces her stories with crystalline laughter

But I'm on to her game, and I know what she's after

There's power within every gaze that she holds

She's found you can "never have too many souls"

Every fool in the room will succumb to her bidding

And I'd say I'm not jealous, but who am I kidding?

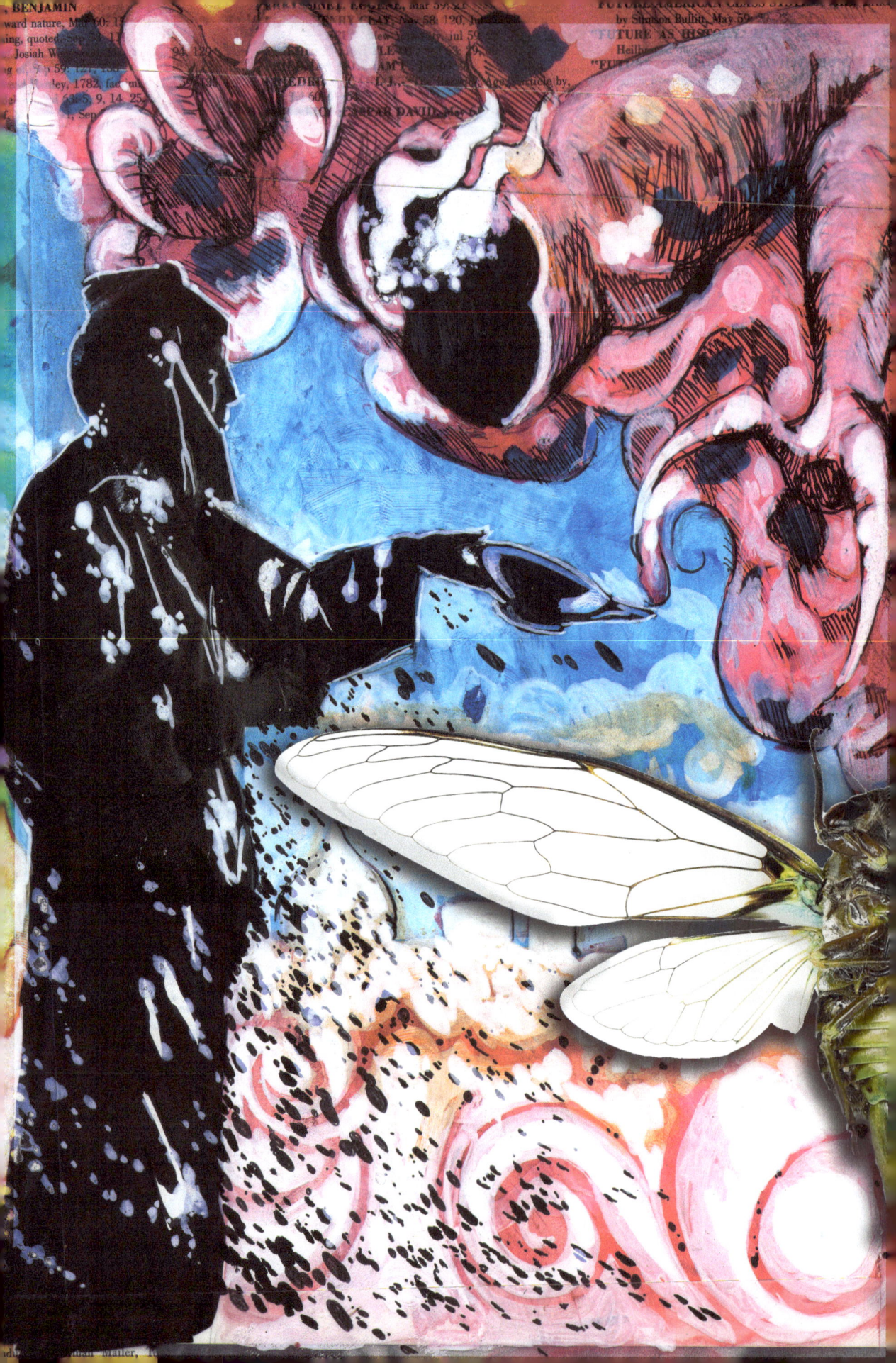

The Wali of Baghdad

The angels came from light but the jinn came from fire, and I asked him if this was why he whispered evil into men's hearts.

"Man's heart is made of clay, and is a vessel to be filled, but they choose which whispers fill them."

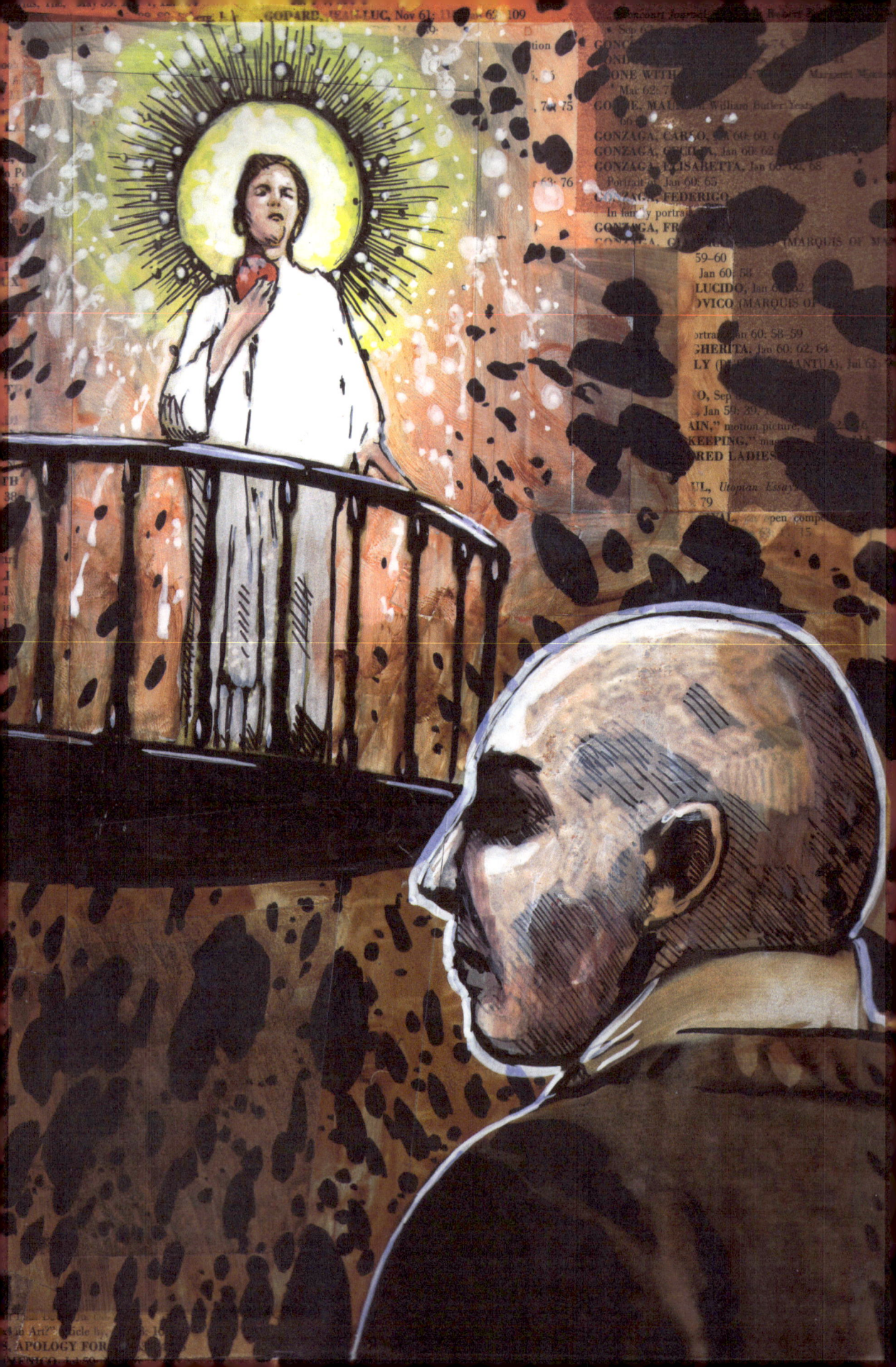

The True Sight of Mayhayley Lancaster

The little girl from the mill
got herself murdered
and murders were hard enough
to divine as it was.
All this talk of guilt and innocence
and "night witches"
made it hard for her to see.

Then they strung Leo up that tree,
and it got even harder.
Muddier
than a red
Georgia river
after a storm.

There's got to be
a better way
to get the truth
from the livin',
rather than waitin'
until they're dead.

But you go to bed blind,
no tellin' where you'll wake up.

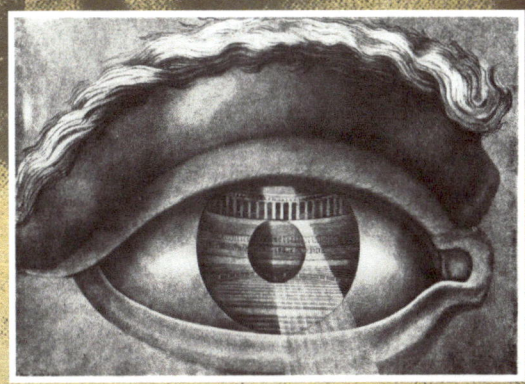

Just ask Justice.

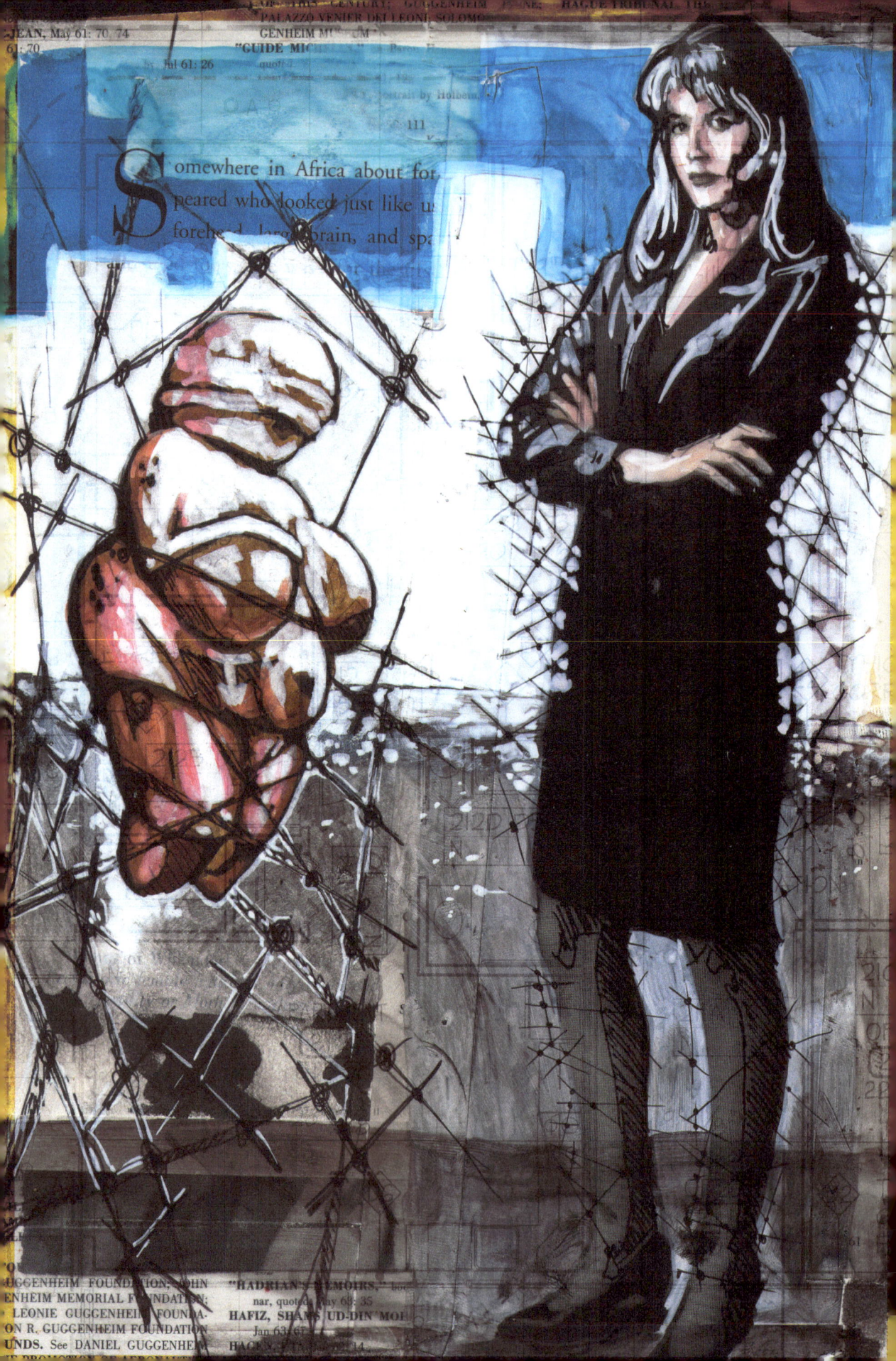

13th Floor Strega

In this crazy, modern, dog-eat-dog world, a girl has to find her way to the top and stay there.

Some might call it nepotism, but it's just an old family tradition.

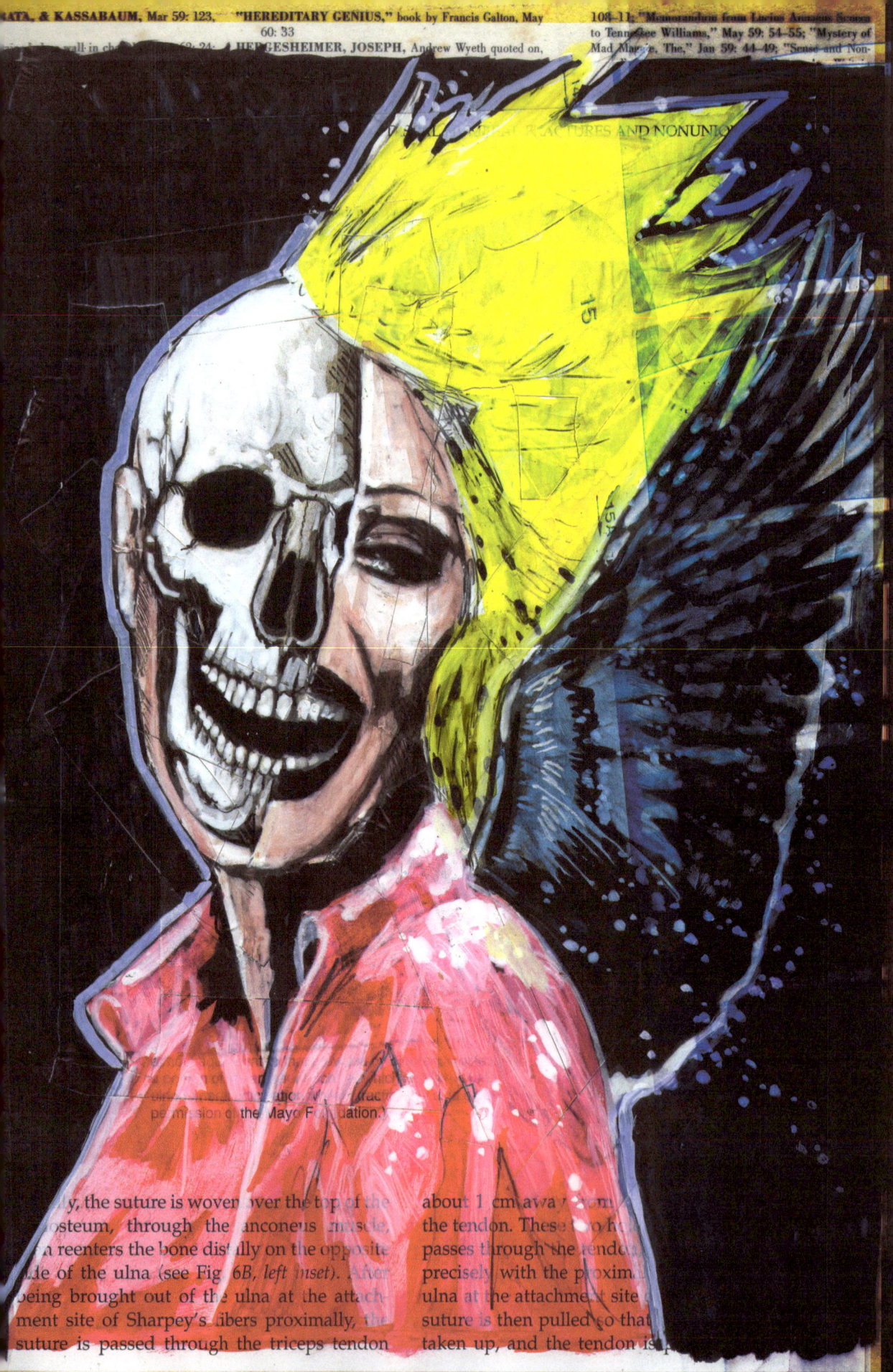

Some Like it Extremely Hot

It would be easy to call this a morality play ~
a young woman, naïve and alone, sells her soul for fame,
fortune, and
adoration.

But sometimes there is no lesson,
no warnings to heed, no dire consequences
of an extravagant life lived, but a simple
design flaw, or faulty wiring.

Some girls are just bound to
burn up when their stars go out.

And if you're gonna burn,
burn brightly.

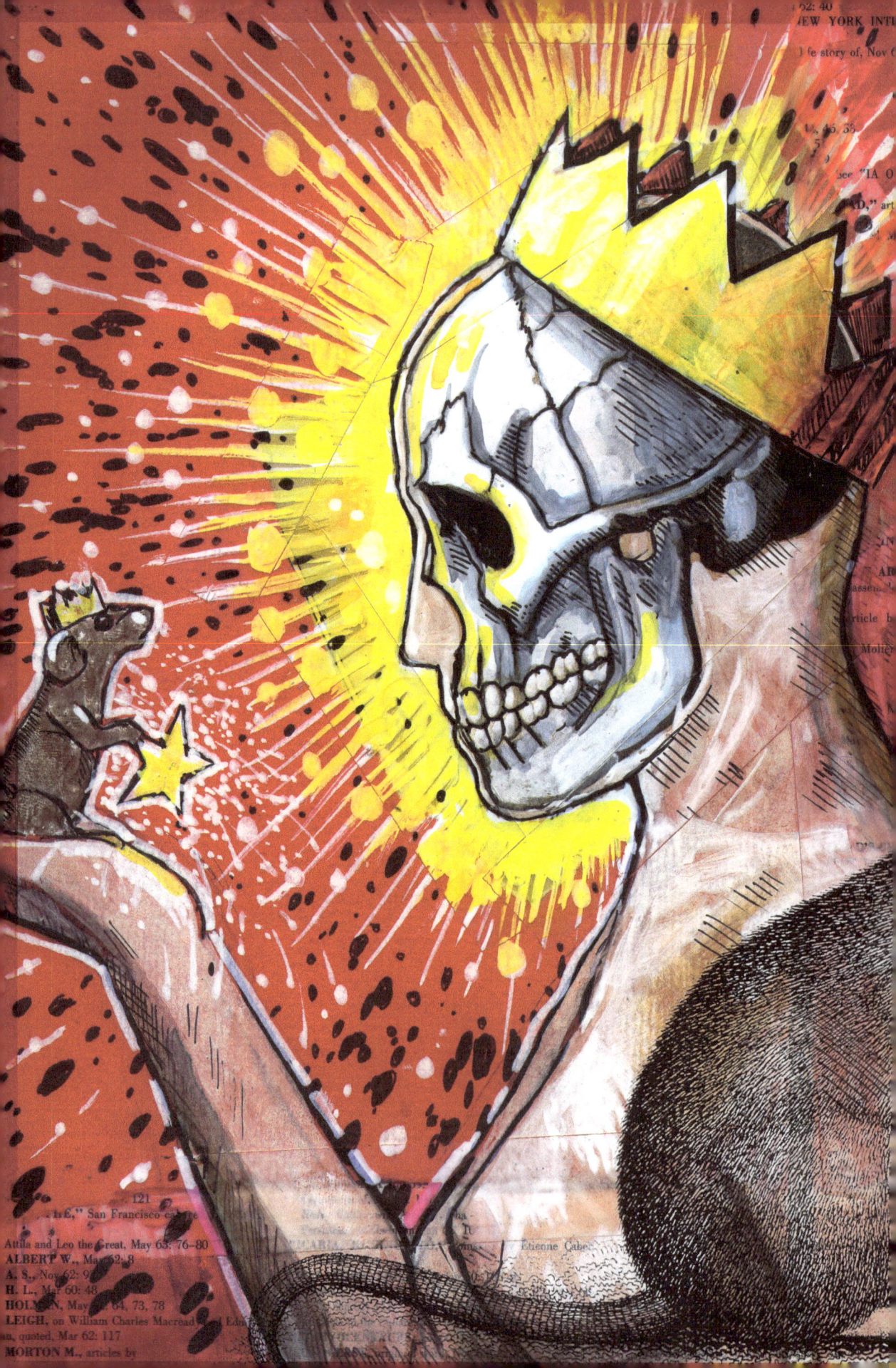

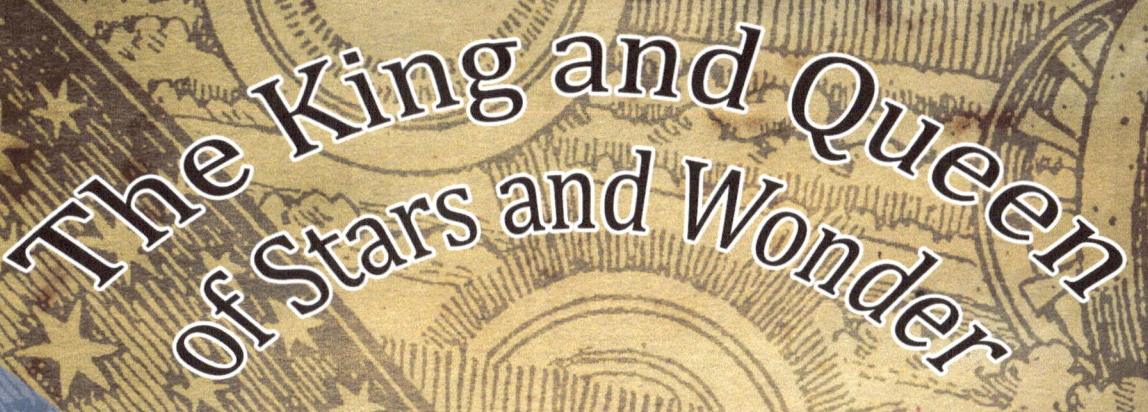

The King and Queen of Stars and Wonder

You be the science,
and I'll be the spectre

You be the wellness,
and I'll be the wraith

You be the law,
and I'll be the lover

You be the future,
and I'll be the faith

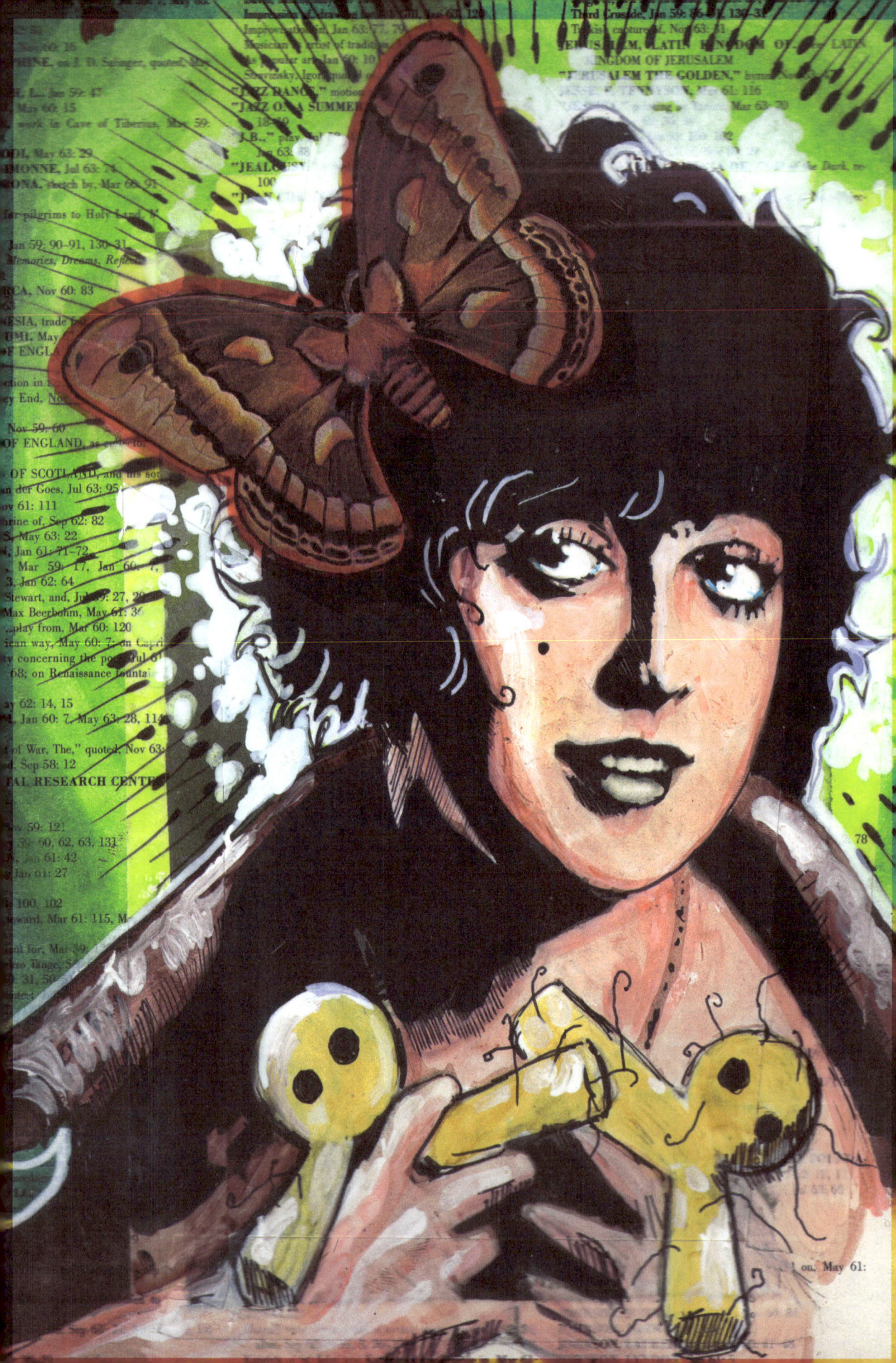

The Dolls
of Bridget Bishop

Those
little poppets
of yours
were no child's play,
but the games of
vicious girls are crueler.

They sold you down the river,
girl, before you even finished
the final stitch,
so next time, throw them
straight into the
fire.

And get rid of the dolls, too.

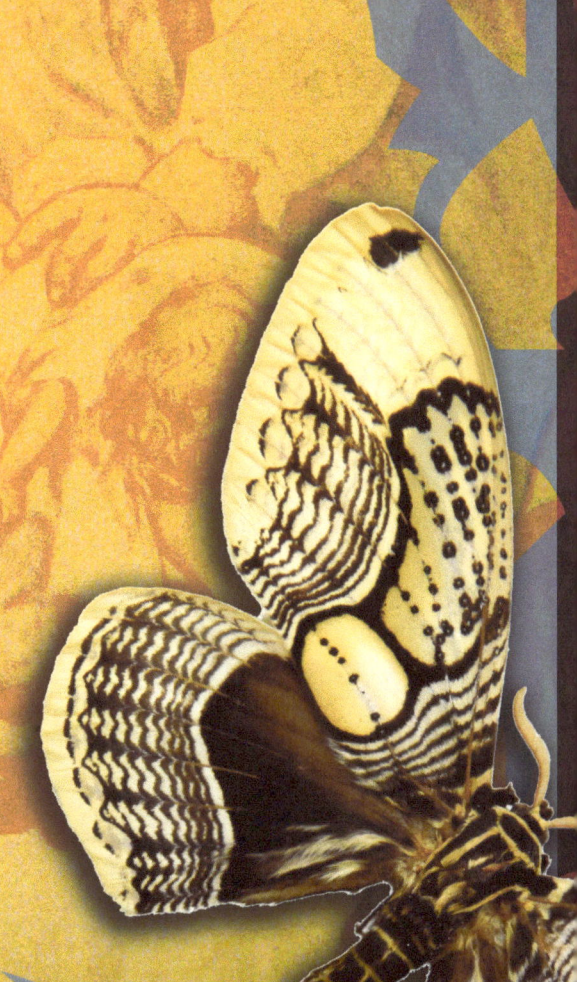

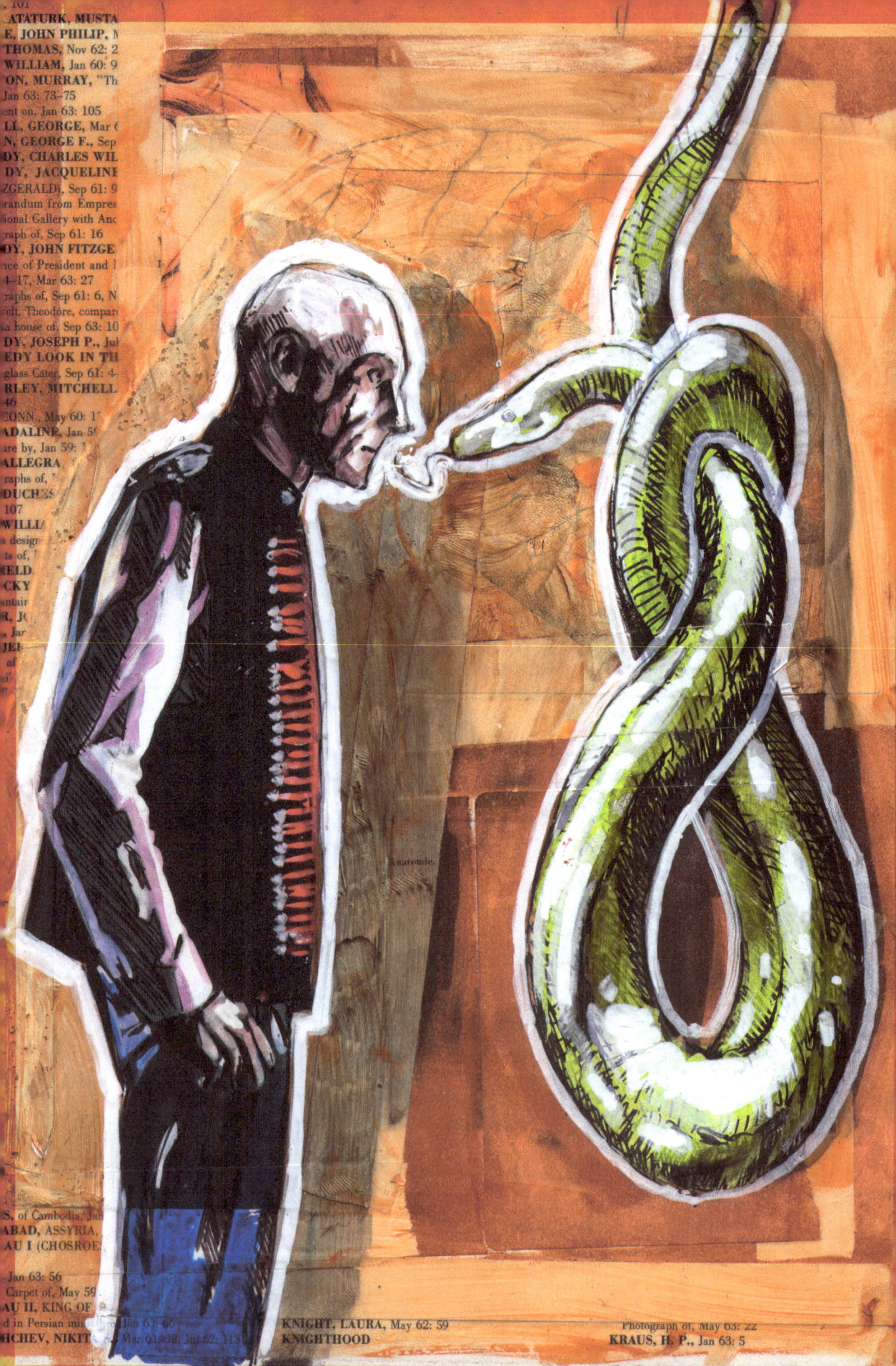

The Road of the Roma Refugees

Was very hidden, indeed
Teach the children to pray to Saint Sarah
Teach them that enemy lines
have got nothing on bloodlines.
Teach them that when a road seems to lead
nowhere, it goes anywhere and everywhere.
Teach them to look to the sea, to look to the sky.
Teach them to flee, teach them to fight.
Teach them to curse.
Teach them to heal.

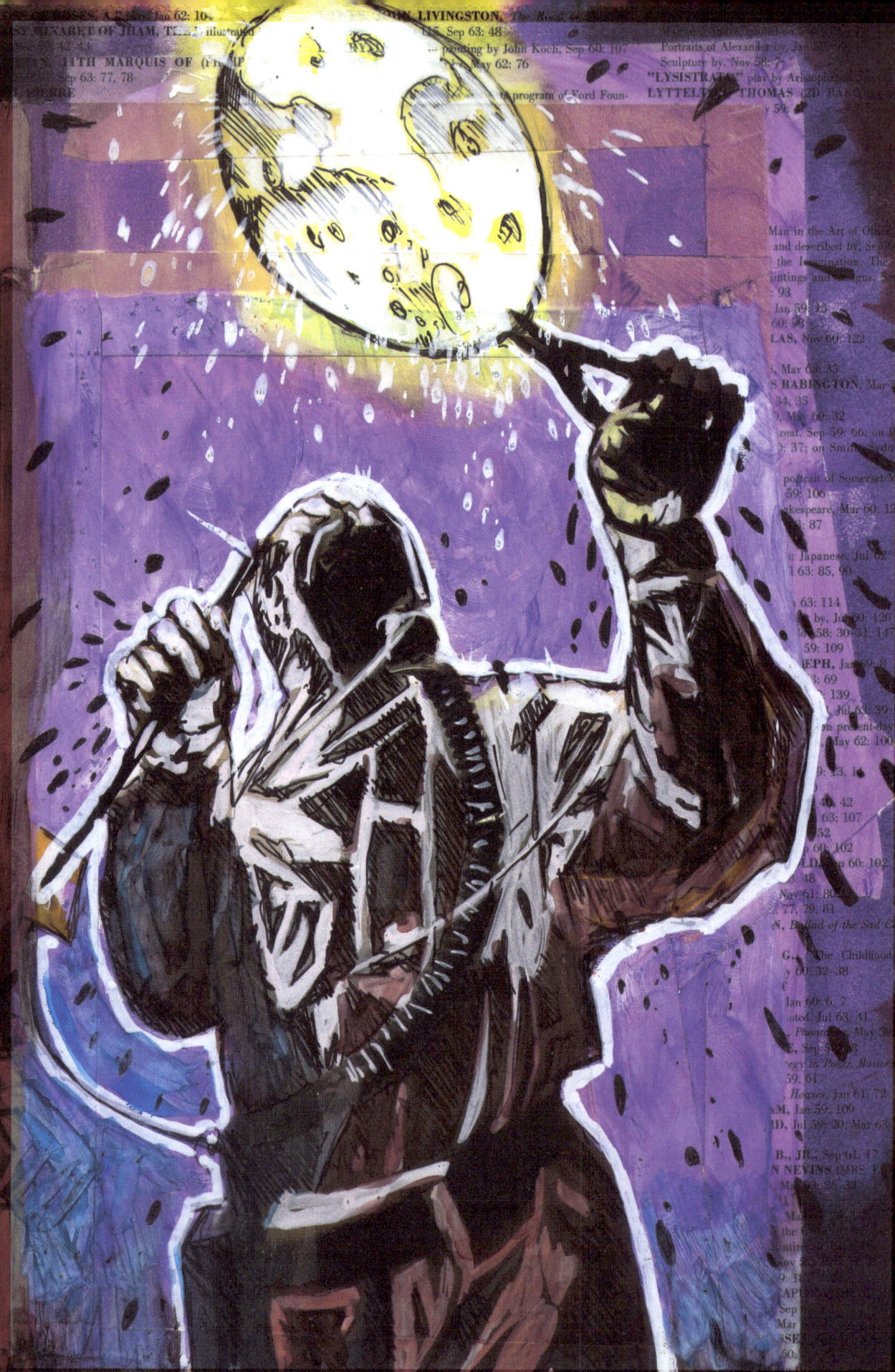

Fukushima
Where We Drew Down the Moon

In a nation of onryō, the moon will never be enough to keep those tides turning.

Her light may never be enough to keep us safe.

僕たちが月をひきずり下ろした福島

怨霊の国。月はもう潮の満ち引きを決めることはできない。
光はもう僕たちを守ることはできない。

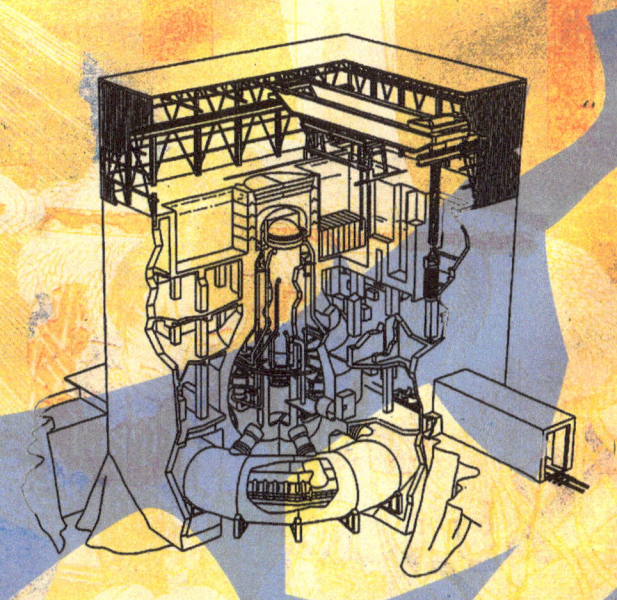

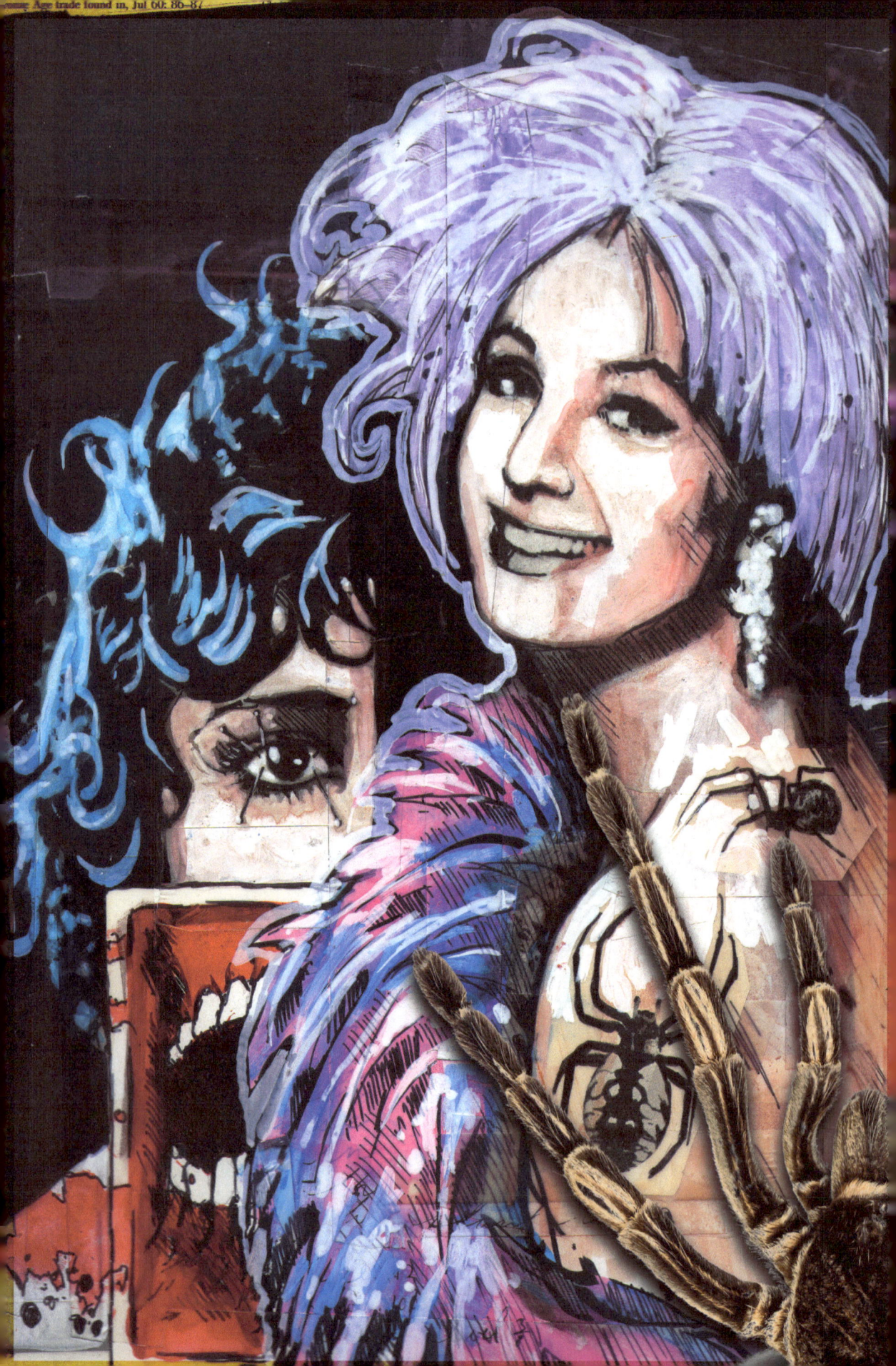

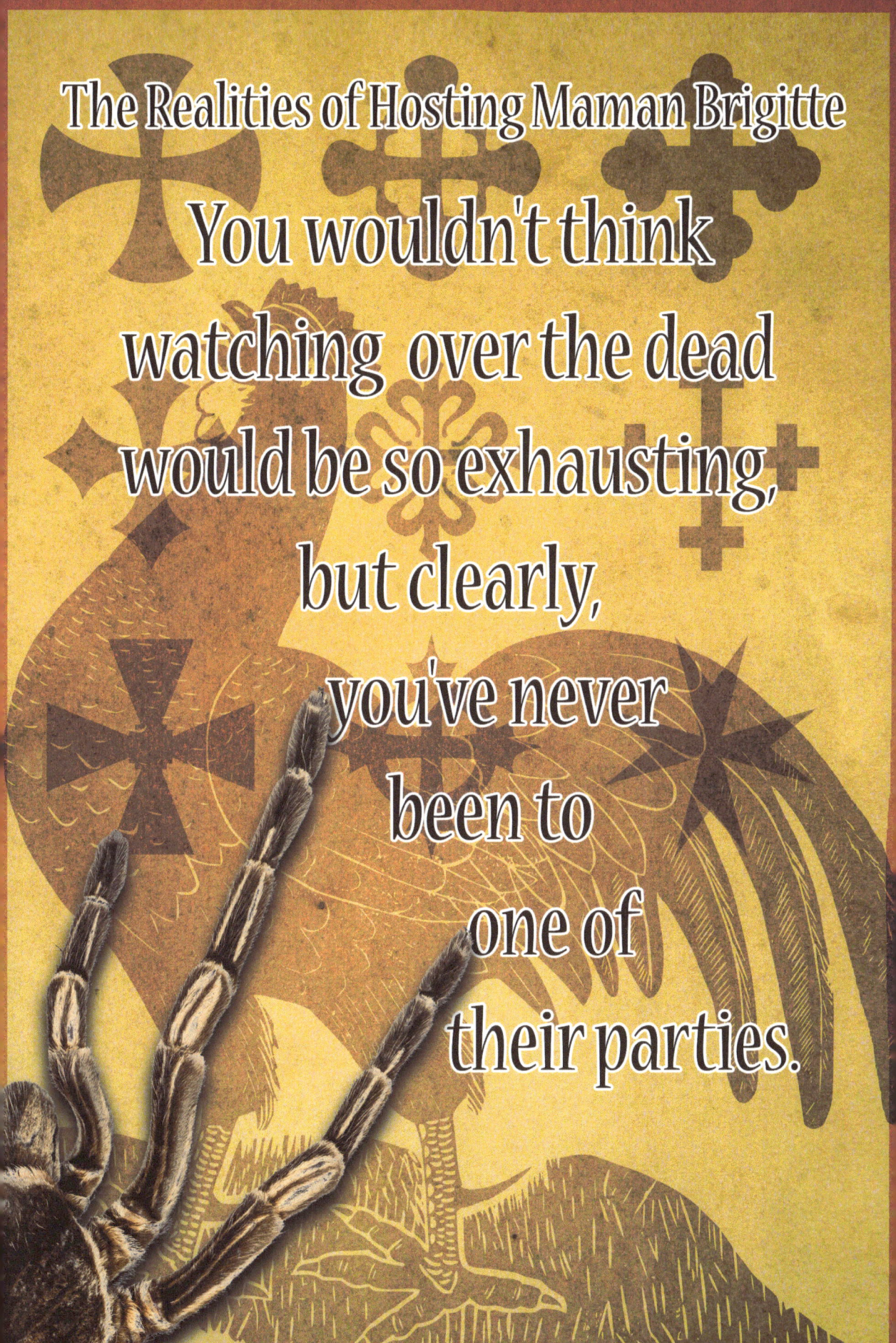

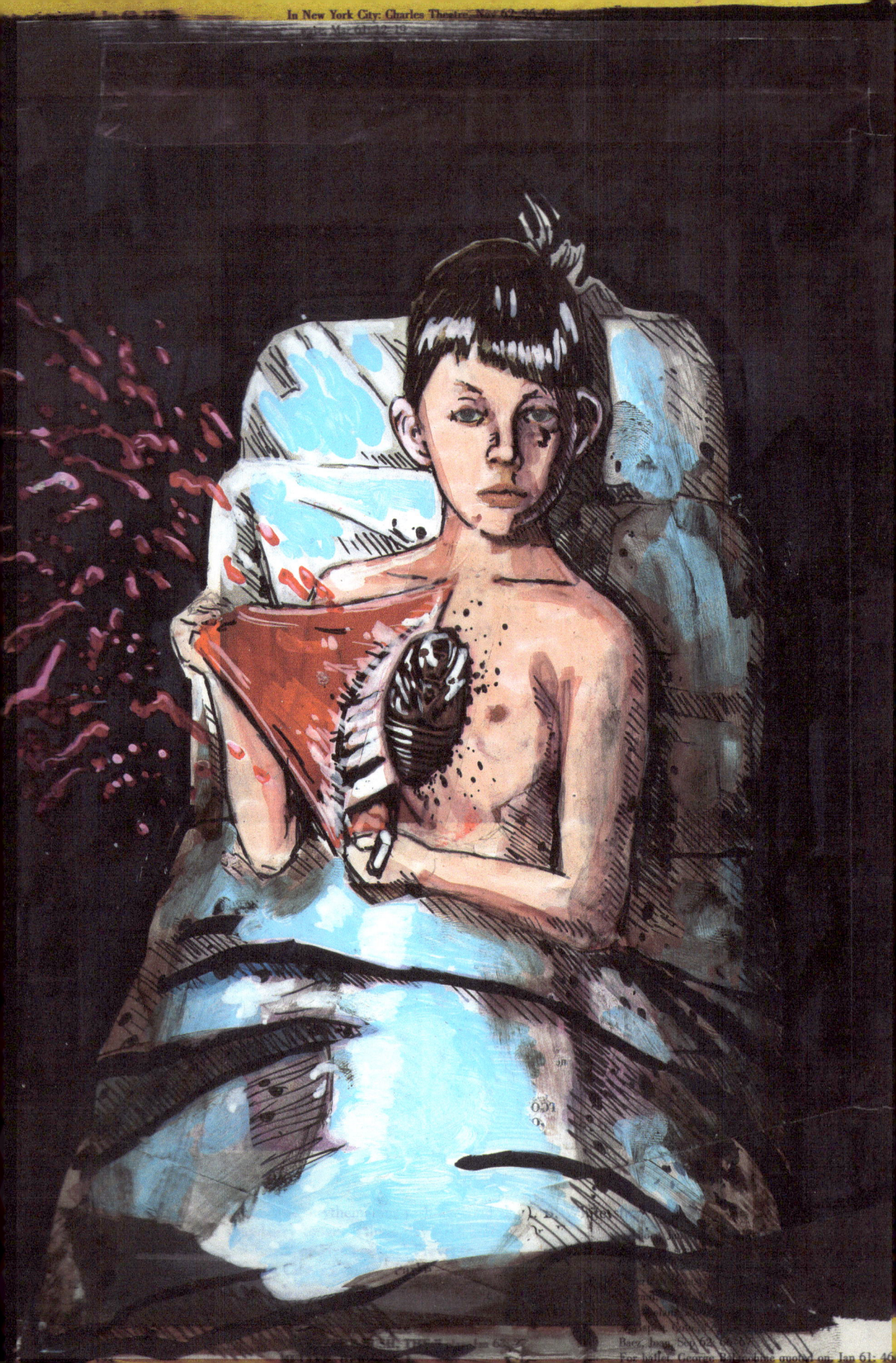

The Billy Witch in Larval Form

With his father at war, his mother
in Pomerania, and Pomerania on fire,
there was no one to keep watch over William.

This was in an early stage of his life,
when his abilities were still in their
infancy, so there was little he could do to
keep the others from torturing him with
terrible games. Their favorite was to
tie a rope to his ankle and make him run
in futile circles,
while they squealed with laughter.

It was not good for William if he refused
to run, so he did, knowing
that one day, things would be very different.
Things within him would be very different,
and
one day
he would return and make sure they knew.

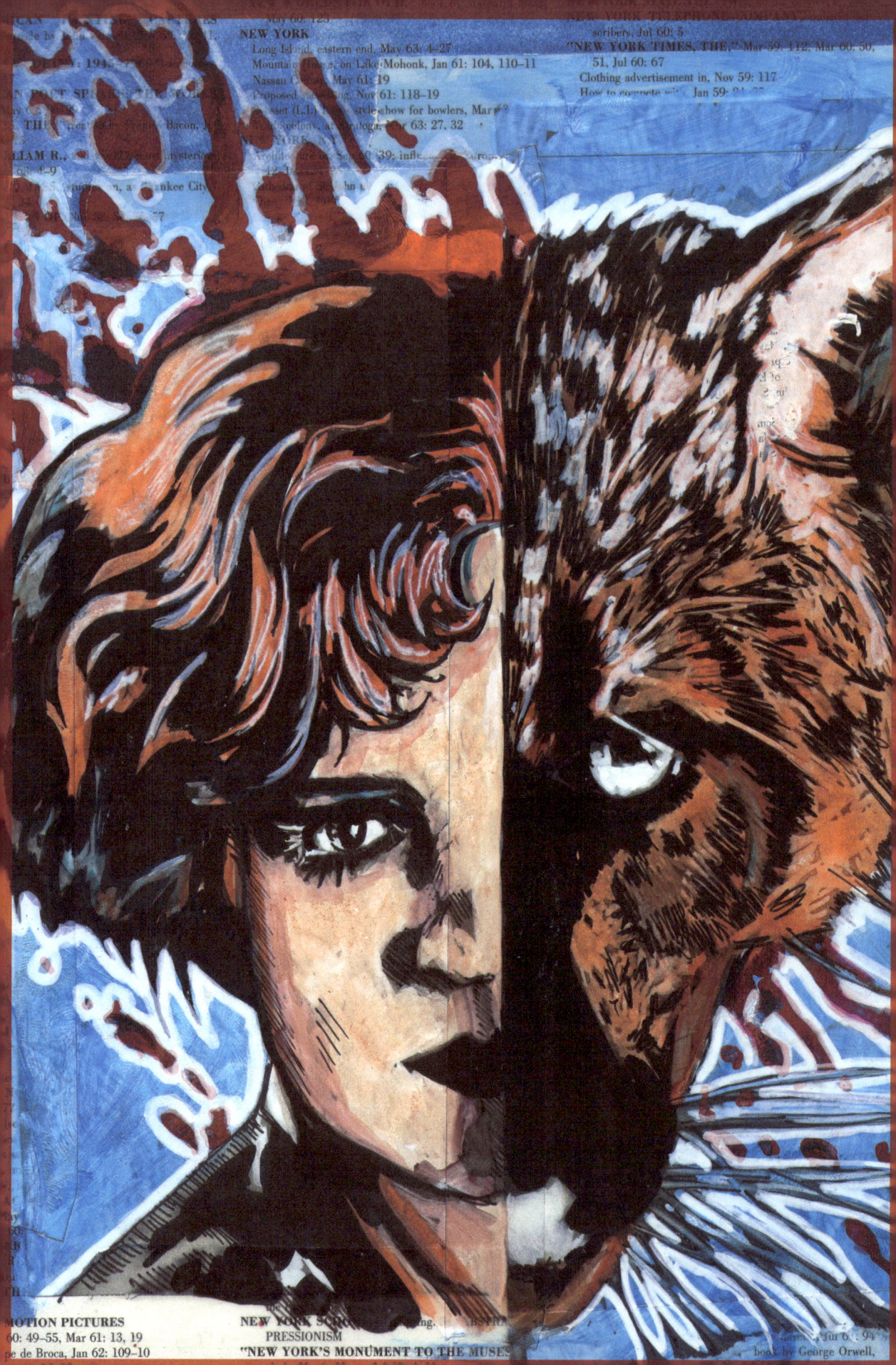

Circe & Her Victims

She changed them to save herself.

She saved herself for last.

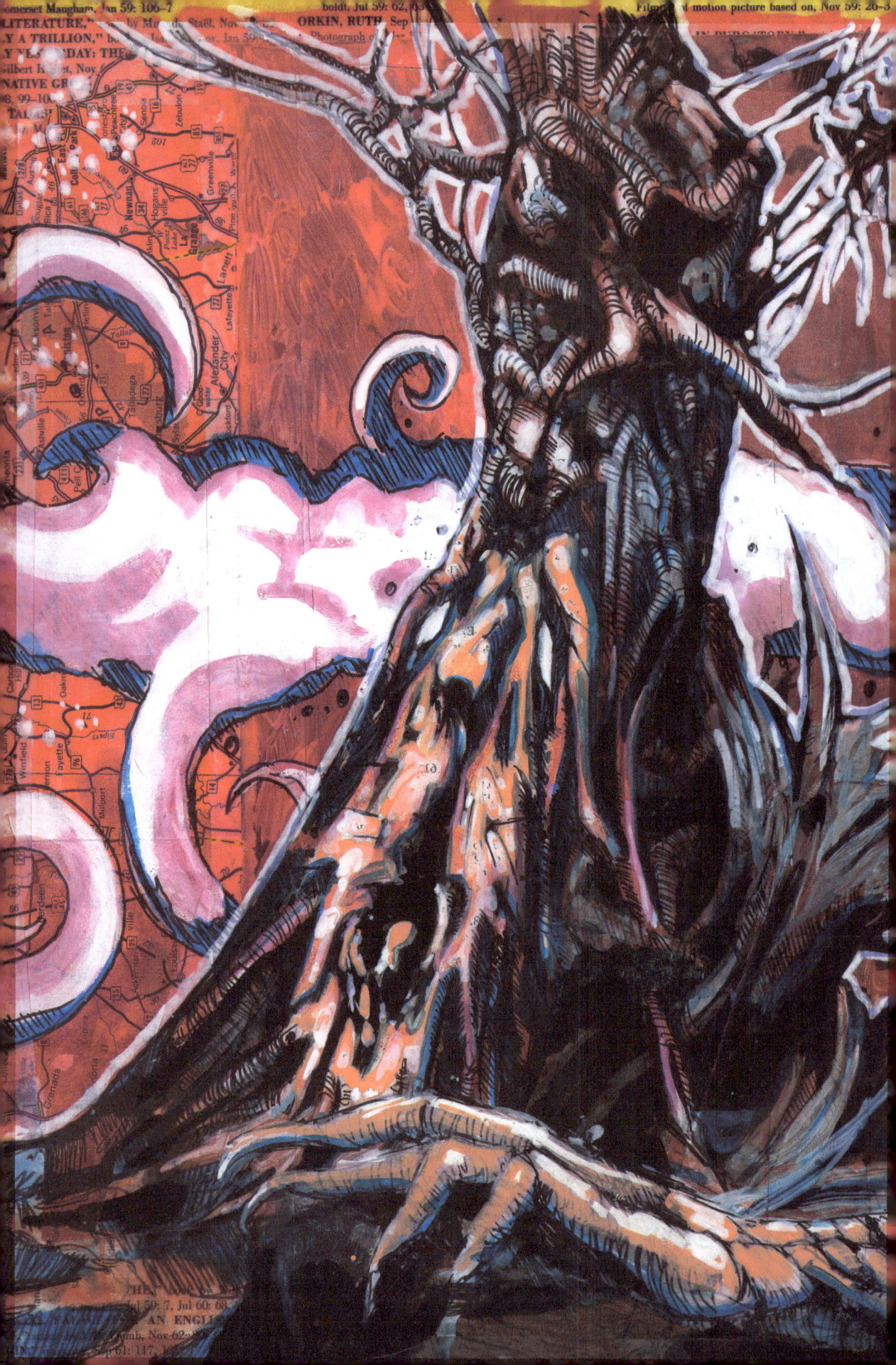

She Who Watches the Lake

She'd seen the terrible things her cousin Wendigo had done ~ the thing he'd become ~ and understood then that even though they'd both made choices that led them to their fates,
they were still choices.

She could not help the
people who walked the land,
or protect them from the beast,
but she could see them safely
across the waters that both
cursed and sustained her.
The same way
the people
cursed and sustained Wendigo.

This is the cycle, she thought.
This is the cycle.

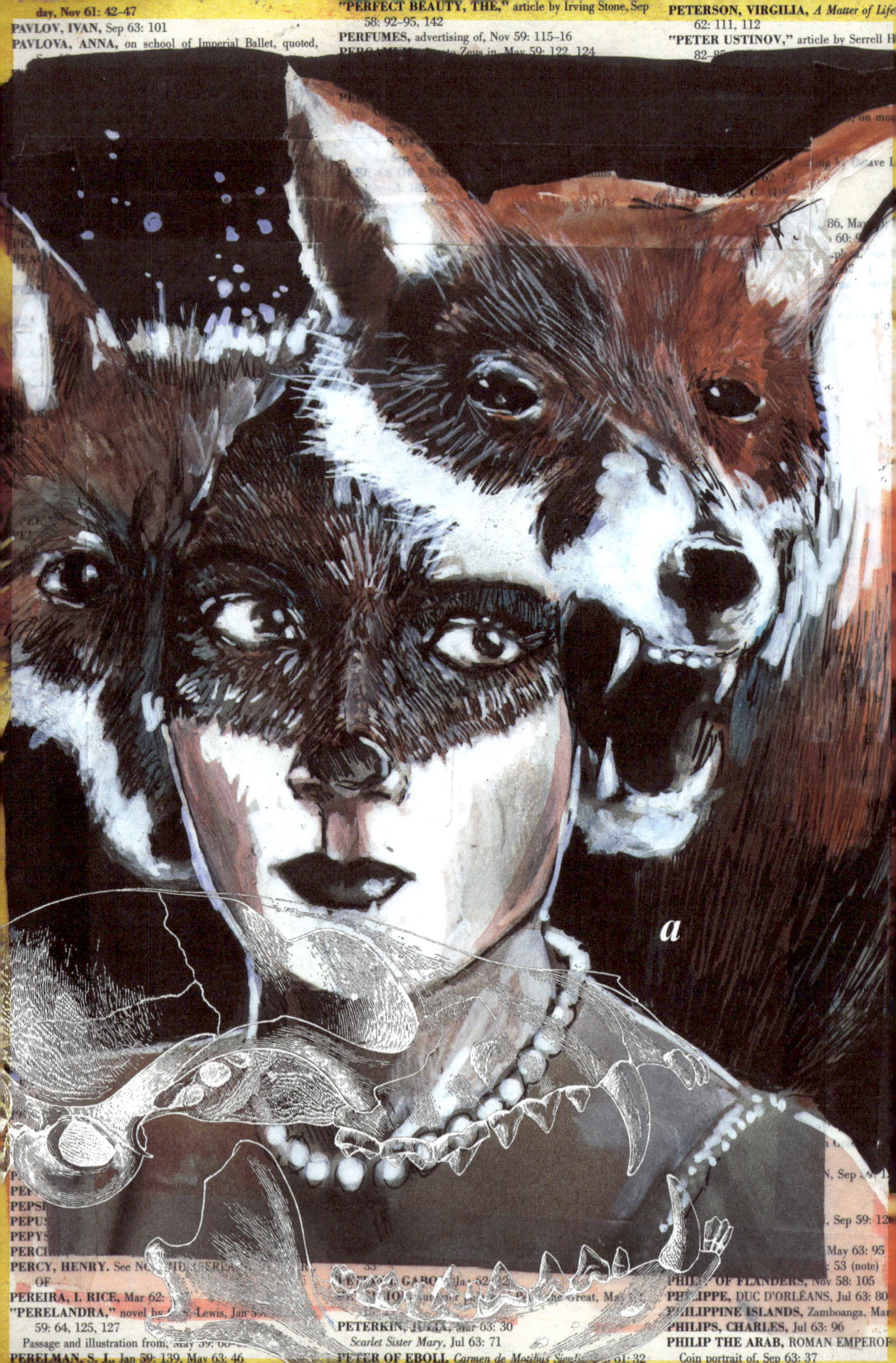

Wrath of the Fox Wife

Everyone thought the Wolf Wives
were worse,
and if you've never
seen a fox
starved of its needs
or never heard their
screaming,
painful curses of sex
and death
coming from the wood,
you might think so, too.

But you'd be wrong.

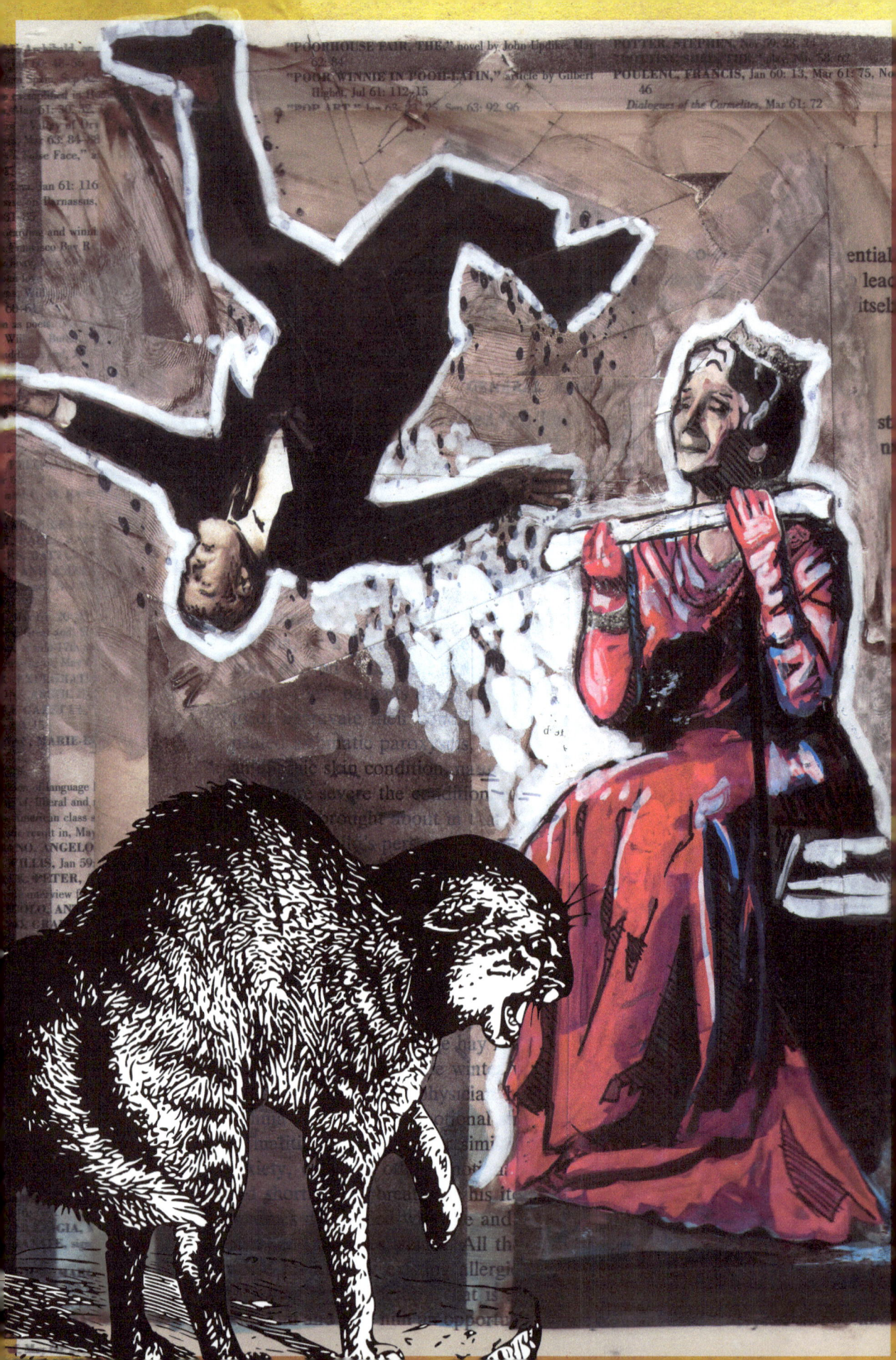

Possibly the Wrong Choice for an Evening's Entertainment

Everyone knew the tricks by that era:
how to make the table levitate and shake,
how to make the candlesticks move,
the automatic writing, the cold readings.
By then it was all done just for a bit of fun.

So imagine everyone's surprise when
Lady Ashton called in the wolves
and made them dance upright like men,
rewarding them after with the organs
and meaty bones of her most pretentious guests.

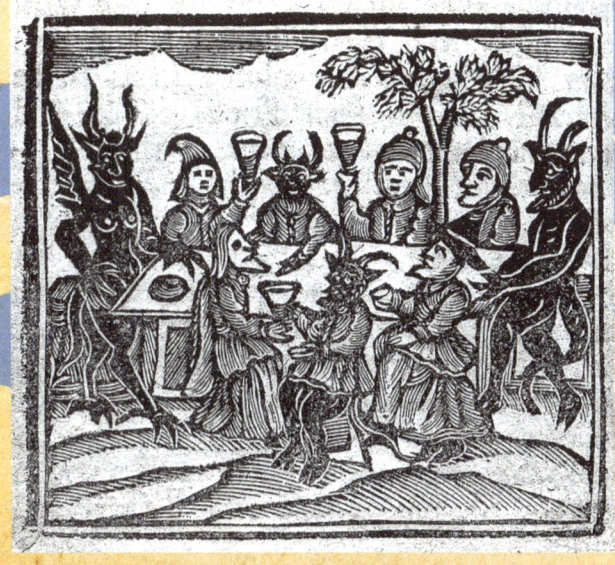

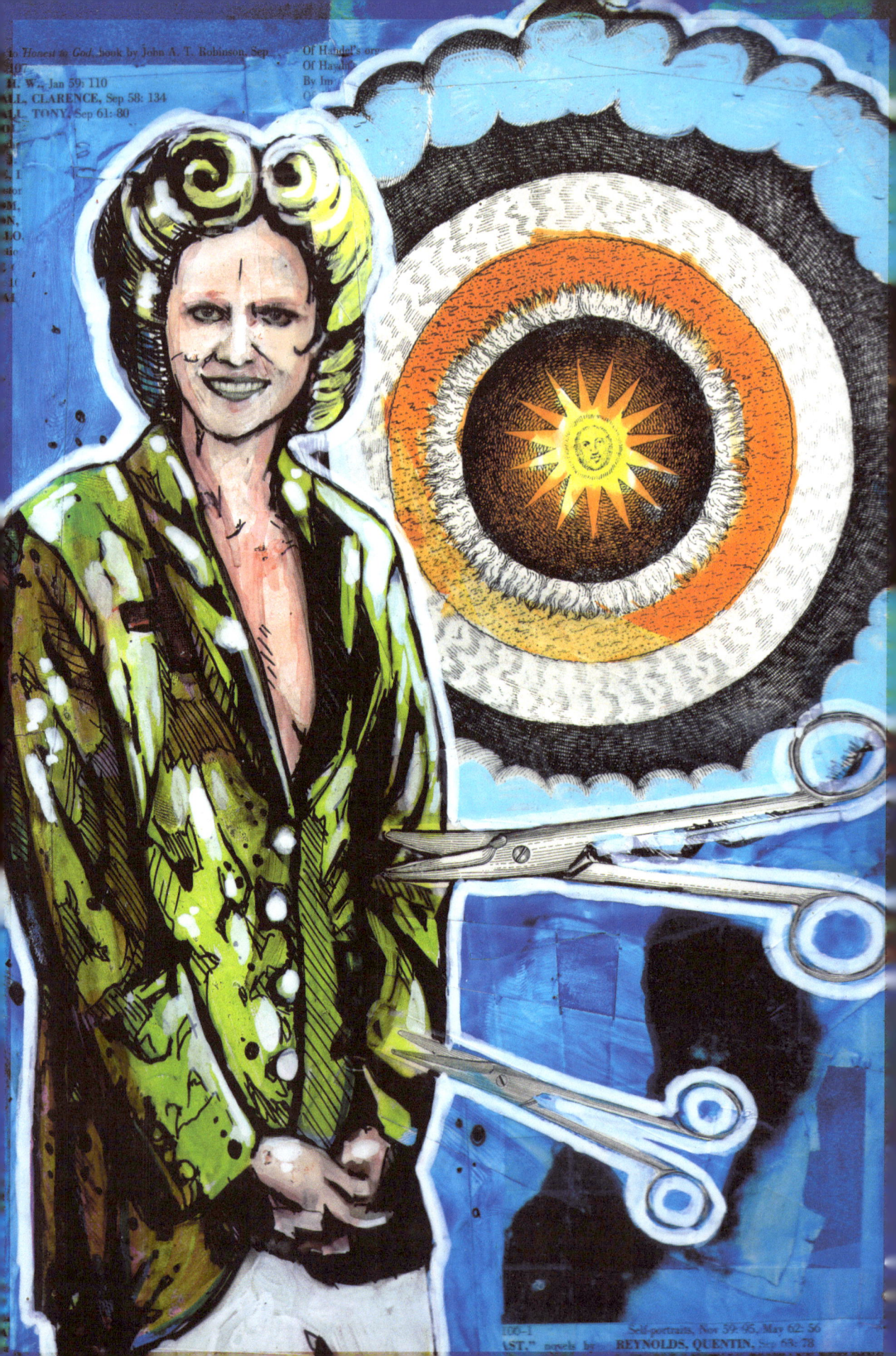

Nurse Exit

Acts of mercy come in many forms.

Think of it as a "spell to mend the painful space you used to inhabit."

It's just finding the right sort of stitch that's a challenge.

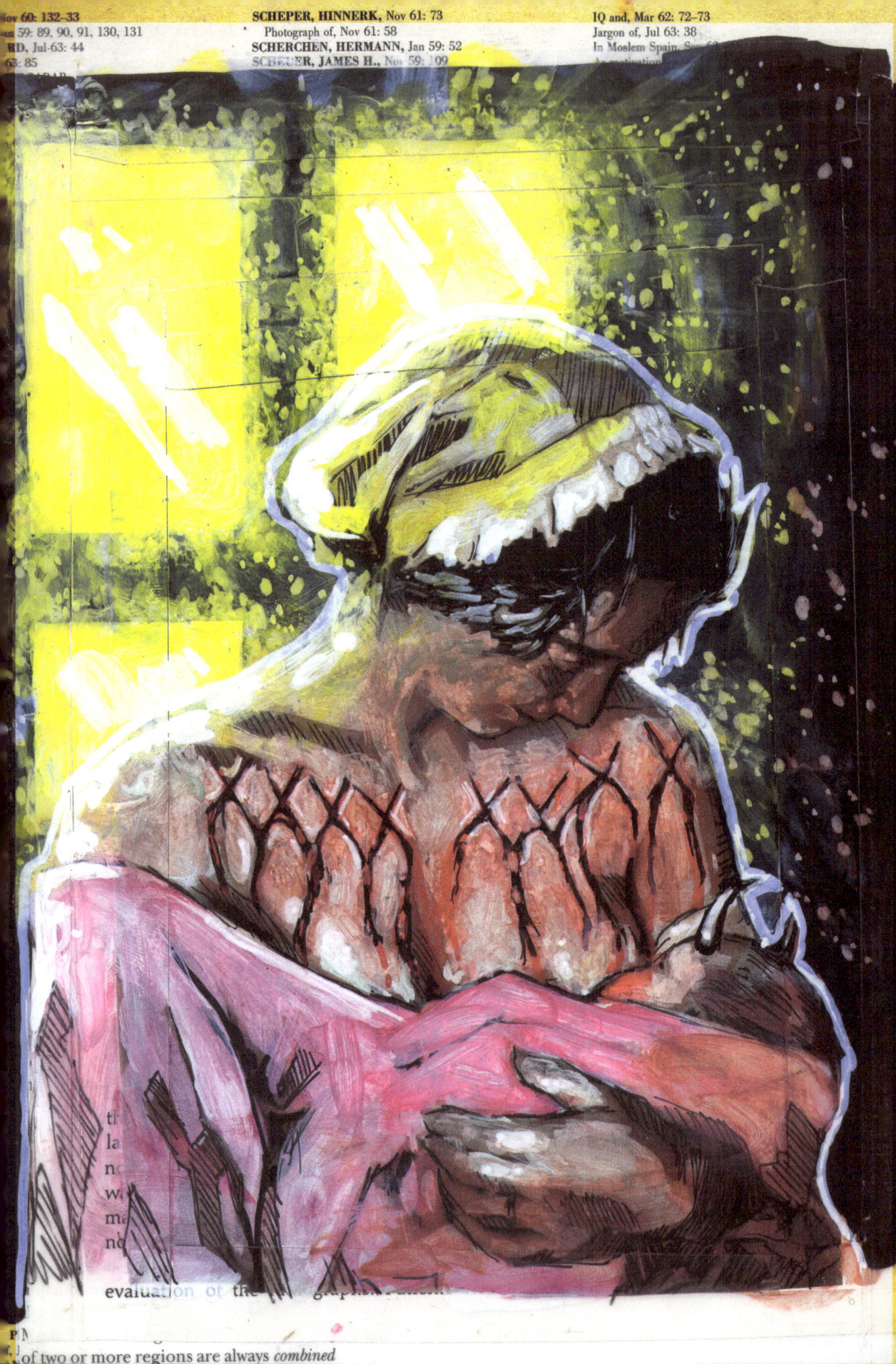

The Adoration of Minnie Castevet

It's a hard lesson, free will. Do you always get to choose what kind of parent you would like to be. And if it takes a village, so be it. No, of course not. But you can choose whether or not you become the vessel for the Antichrist?

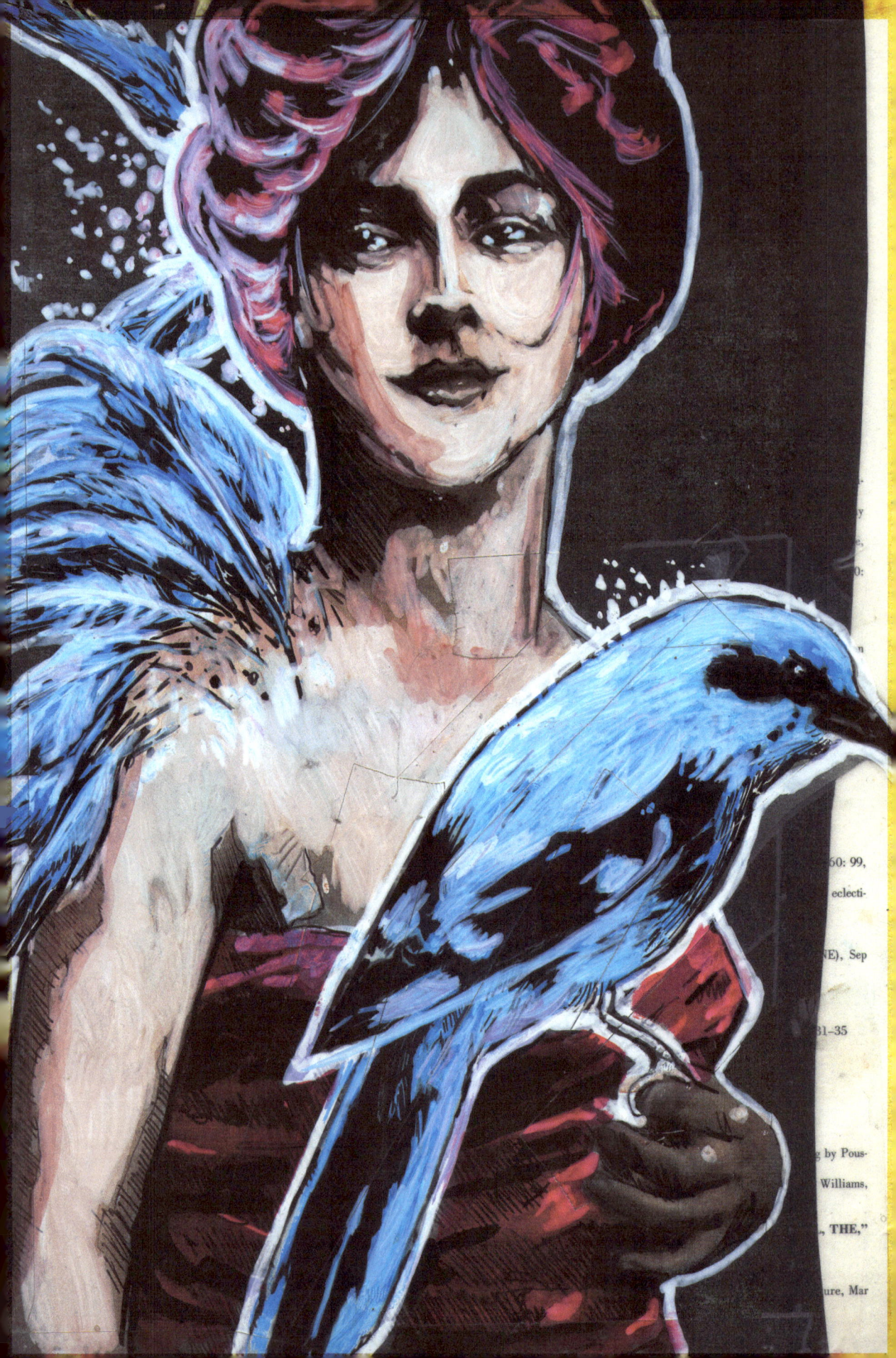

Jezebel's Exit

After the first go round,
the ladies
in the secret court of Baal
made sure to give her wings.

The higher up the window,
the better,
she thought
of air currents
and
graceful displays.

And the dogs?
Well,
they'd just have to go hungry that day.

"High Modern," The," Sep 59: 4–21
San Francisco, The," Jan 59: 4–23
deral Façade," Jan 60: 18–27, 119–21
" Sep 60: 57–69, 72, 81

Circle in the Square, New York City, Mar 60: 94–99, 119–21
Corey, Orlin and Irene, and their theatre, Jan 63: 88–91
Crawling Arnold, play by Jules Feiffer, Nov 61: 49–56

THEODOSIUS III, BYZANTINE EMPEROR, Nov 63: 26
"THEORY OF THE COIFFURED LASSES, A," drawings by Marcello Mariotti, Mar 63: 118–19
"THERE SHALL BE NO NIGHT," play, May 62: 6, 8

ire, Jan 62: 66–71
ory, Mar 61: 44, 46
used for performances, Jul 62: 27–31
and his plays, Nov 60: 50–55, 126–27
ct 62: 68, 71

by Gilbert Highet, May 60: 126–28
THEOCRITUS, in Renaissance curriculum, Jan 60: 6
THEODORA, BYZANTINE EMPRESS, Sep 60: 126, Nov 63: 10, 11, 12
Portrait of, Nov 63: 18–19

THUR , L. L., Ma 62: 71
THYN E, THOMAS, house of, Nov 58: 38–39
TIAMAT, Mesopotamian deity, Jul 61: 37

Sycorax

There is
no greater,
lasting force
~ nurturing or destructive ~
than
a mother's
love.

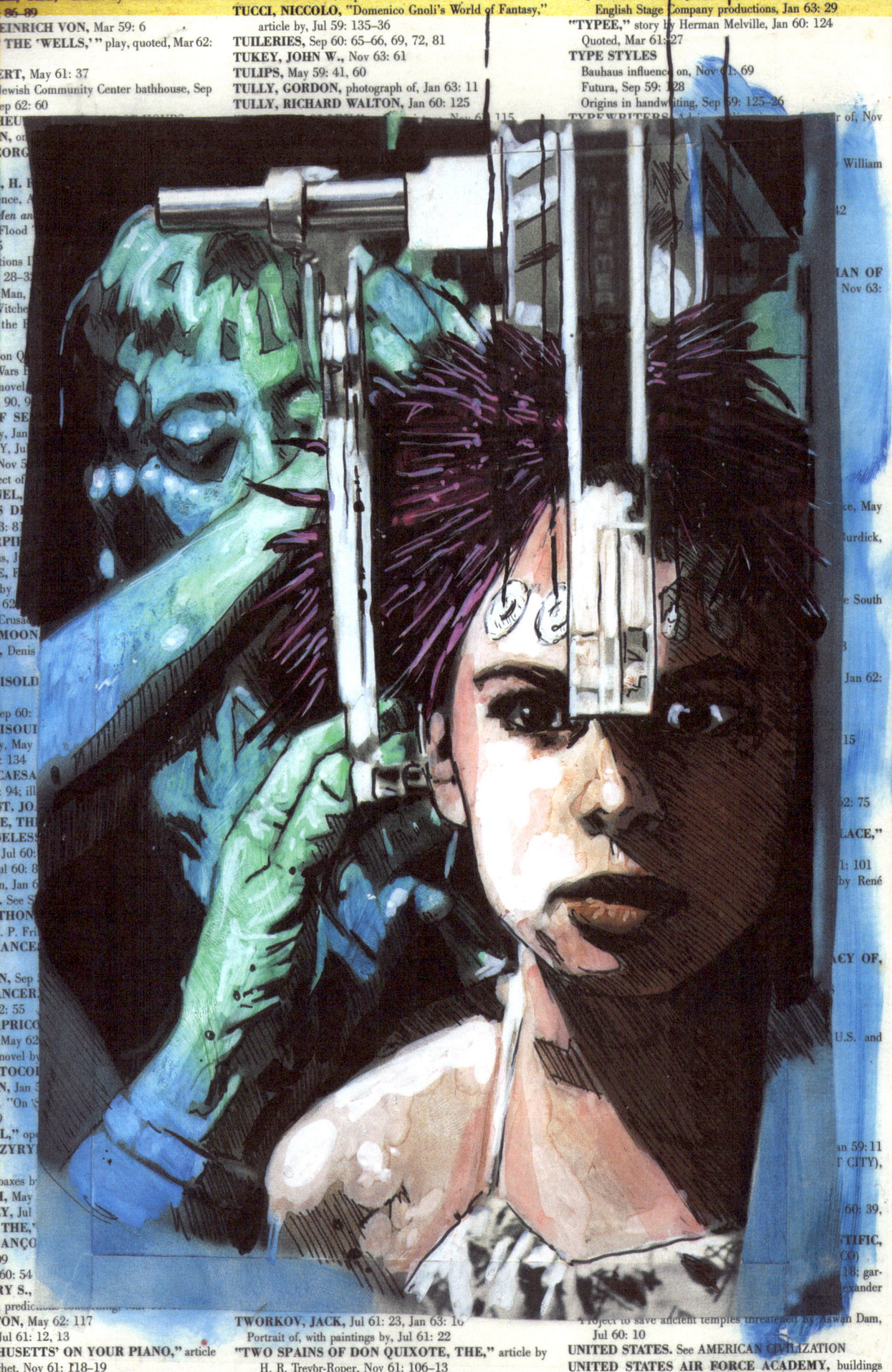

Clarissa, Whose Evil Could Not Be Measured

You can't help her. Not within this paradigm.

Try to build a stable, unchanging shelter in a place with winds, with floods, with droughts, with blizzards, with scorching heat.

In some societies, the voices she hears are whispered warnings and are welcomed. In others, the same voices are perceived as screaming threats.

In some societies, the voices are ancestors and guardians. In others they are demons. And in ours they are a flaw in the design.

There are things she destroys that need destroying. Rotting from the inside and no longer safe.

But you'd only know that if you'd seen the rot.

And if you never saw it, you might be inclined to question how bad it really was, if it existed at all.

Pitiful creatures such as her never stand a chance. No charm, no healing spell will take. Nor do the hexes.

There is no magick here.

Only chemicals and the way they spill into her brain, and onto the world.

Only the chemicals that spill onto her out of other people's brains, coming through their hands and their bodies and

their words.

Witches, take heed...

You never need those herbs, those stones, those lengths of twine.

You need only words.

And there's no greater curse than too many variables.

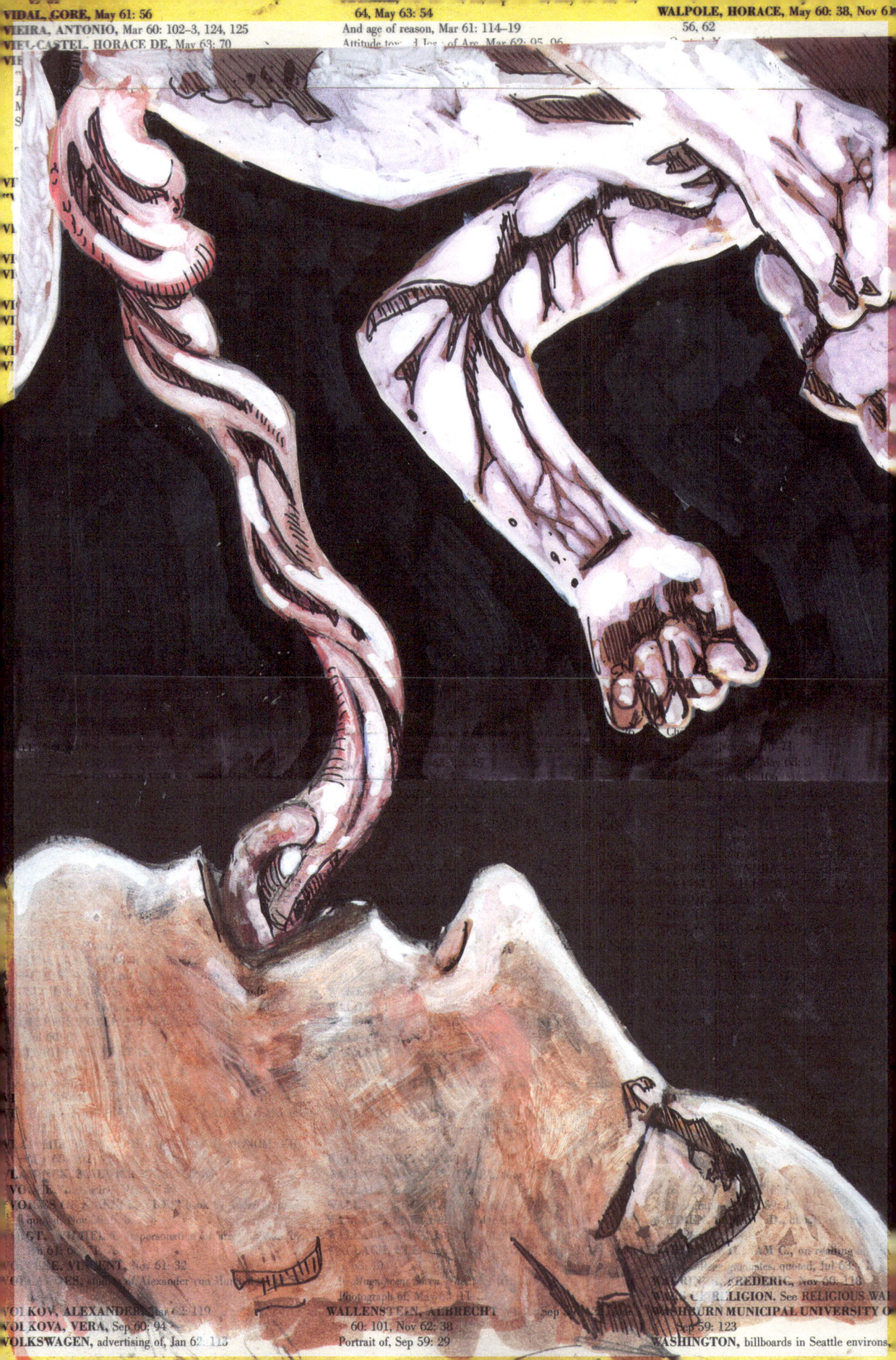

Sleep and Dream of Keziah Mason

There was no place too far or hidden
that she would not go to serve her devil

Her name in the book sealed her commitment

So what does it say that she's calling to you
through folds of space and consciousness?

How far are you willing to go?

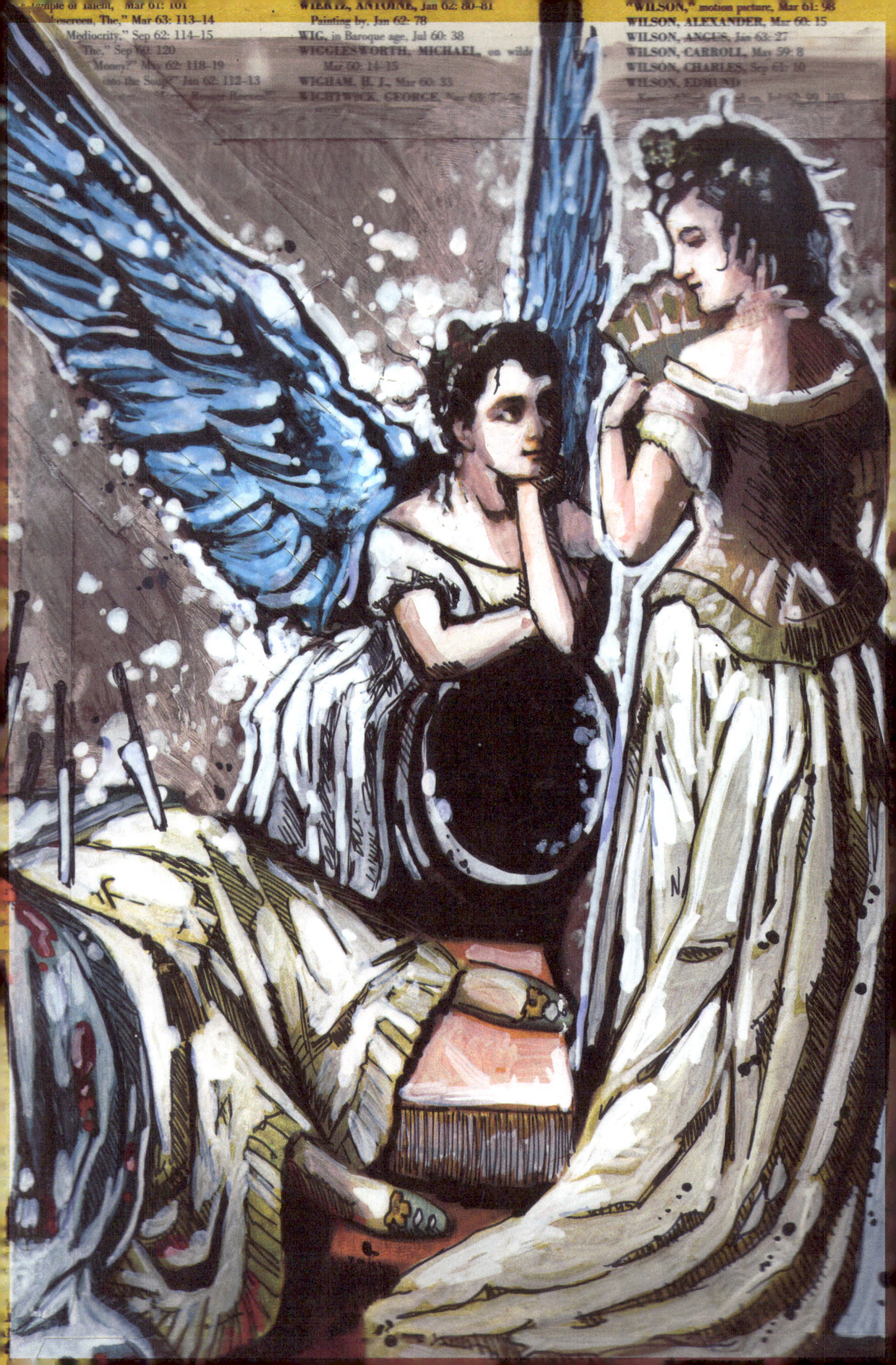

The Harpy

From the unit, she could see through wire
mesh-encased windows, the forest
where her winged sisters fed.

Though the sisters were hungry, she
could not force the hands of the lost,
only encourage them to follow through with
unfinished business.

The forest was beautiful, she'd tell them.

Their souls would live in the trees.

No more grief.

No more lingering in the cold,
locked wards—these earthly preludes to the
Seventh Circle.

And while all these things were true
in the Wood of the Self-Murderers,
Nurse Celaeno would forever neglect to
mention the pain of being stripped
of your new leafy flesh by clawed feet
and slowly devoured, entombed in swollen,
feathered bellies.

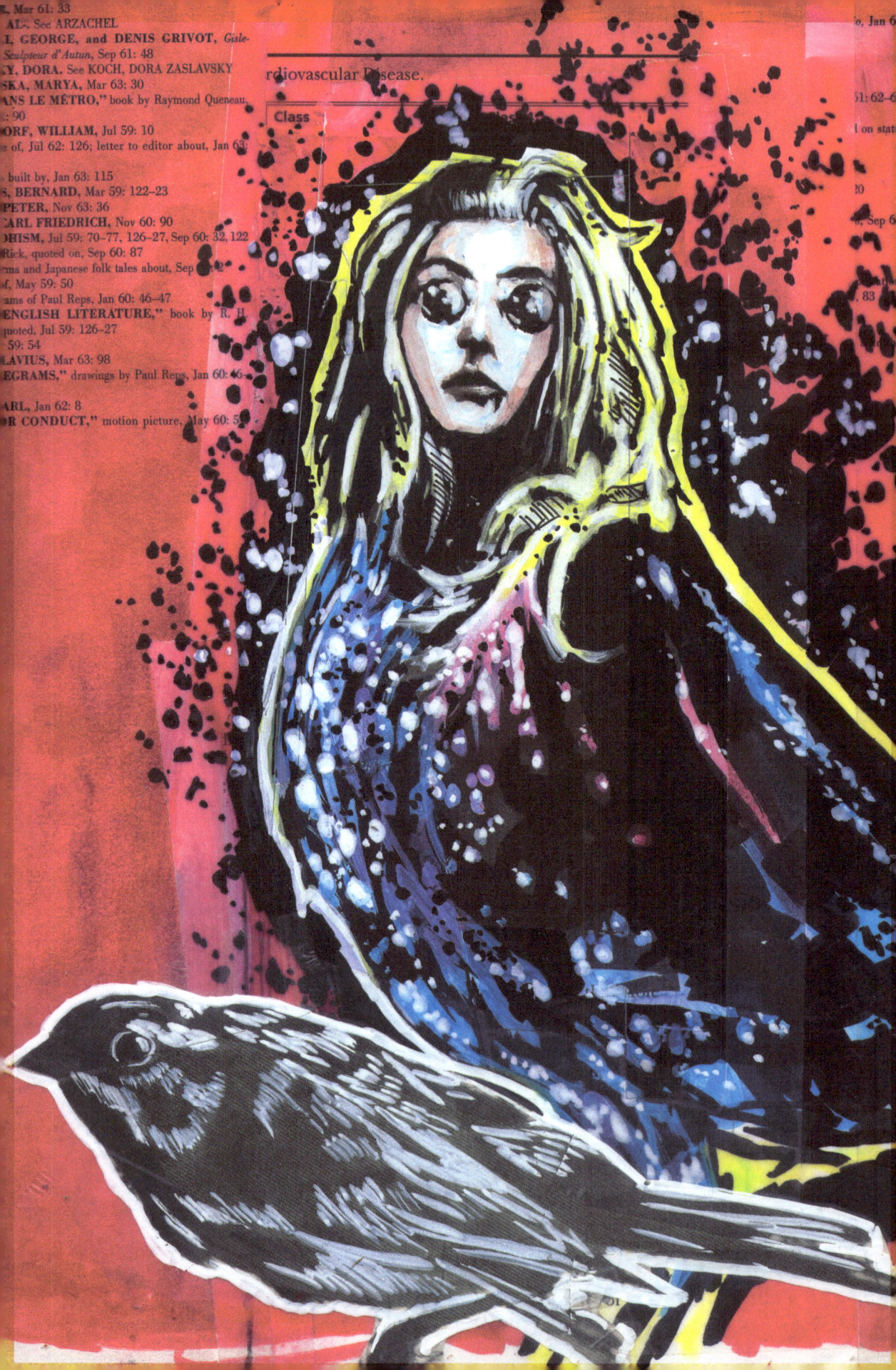

The Family, Familiar

Sisters and brothers
who swear allegiance
to the foxes
and corvids, the wolves
and the serpents,
the felines and
rodents:

Servant or master,
soldier or General...
do you know which one you are?
Are you sure?

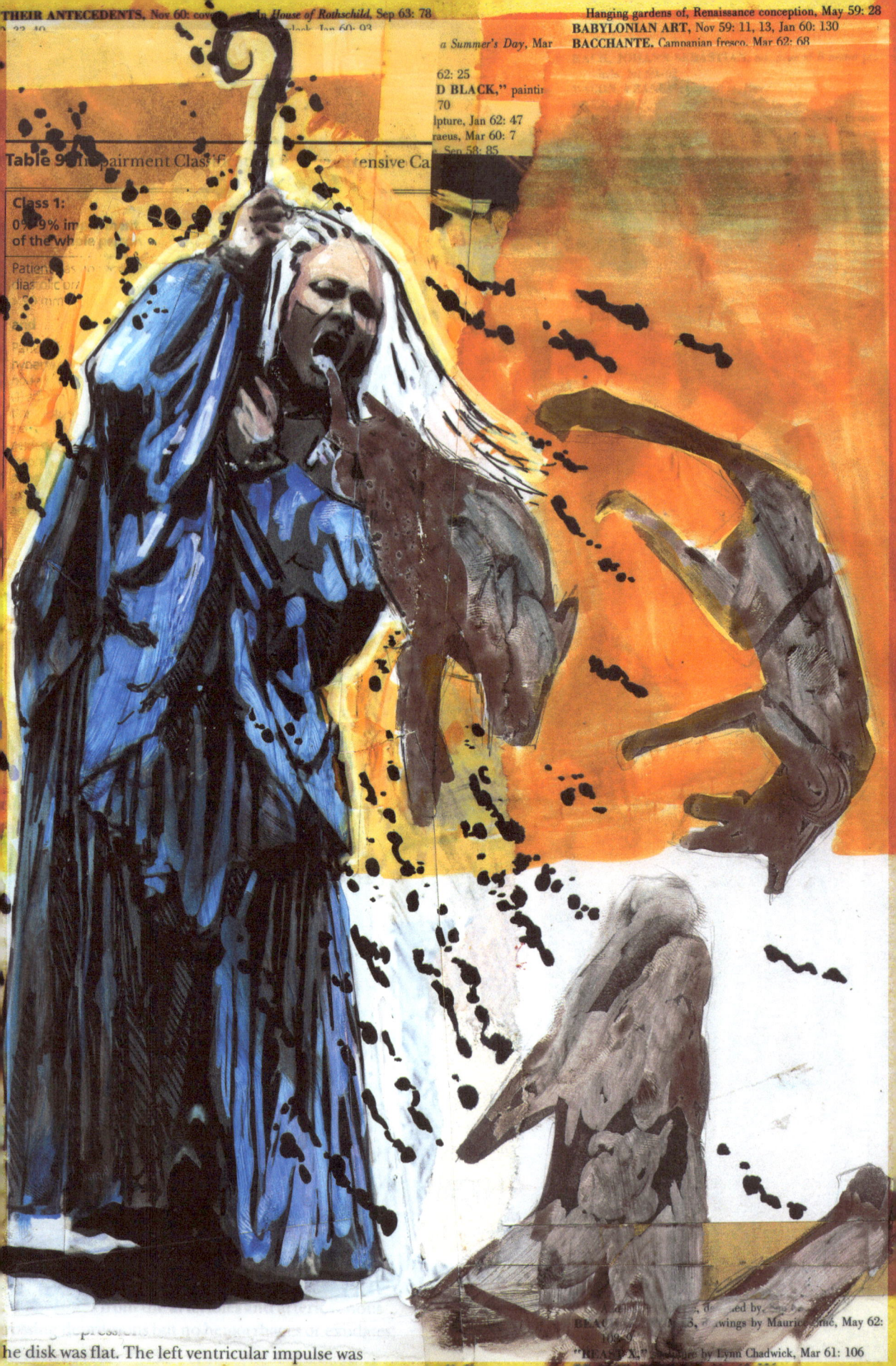

Mother Tundra

You do her a great disservice
by imagining
she is only cold,
dry death.
Her wind-chapped
skin and bones may be
permanently frozen,
but in her heart
there are shallow lakes,
black blood,
and fires.
There is life.
Her children
must be strong
and adaptable,
unlike any others,
with fires in their hearts
for when all else
is cold and dark.

Because the cold and dark will always come.

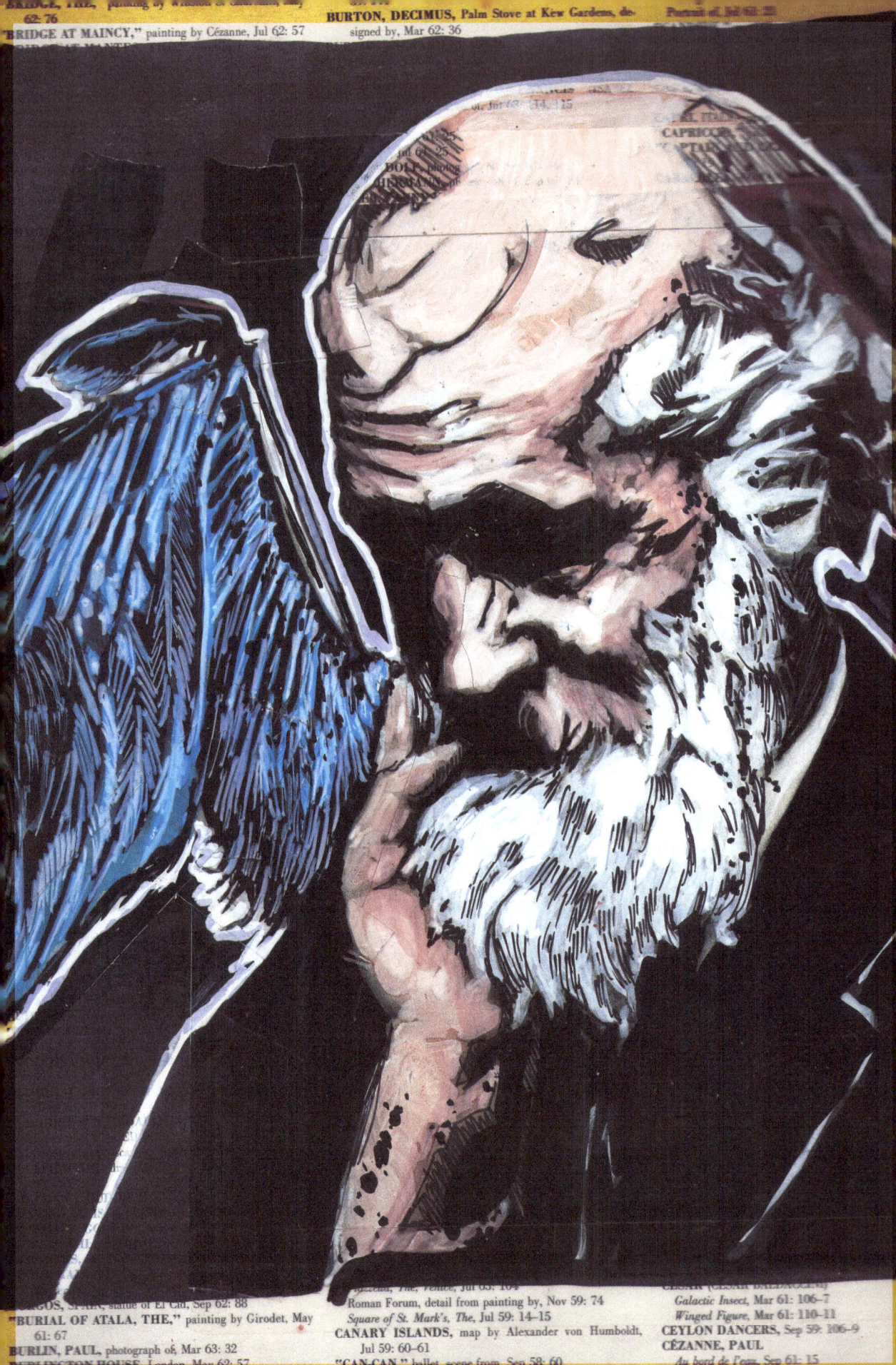

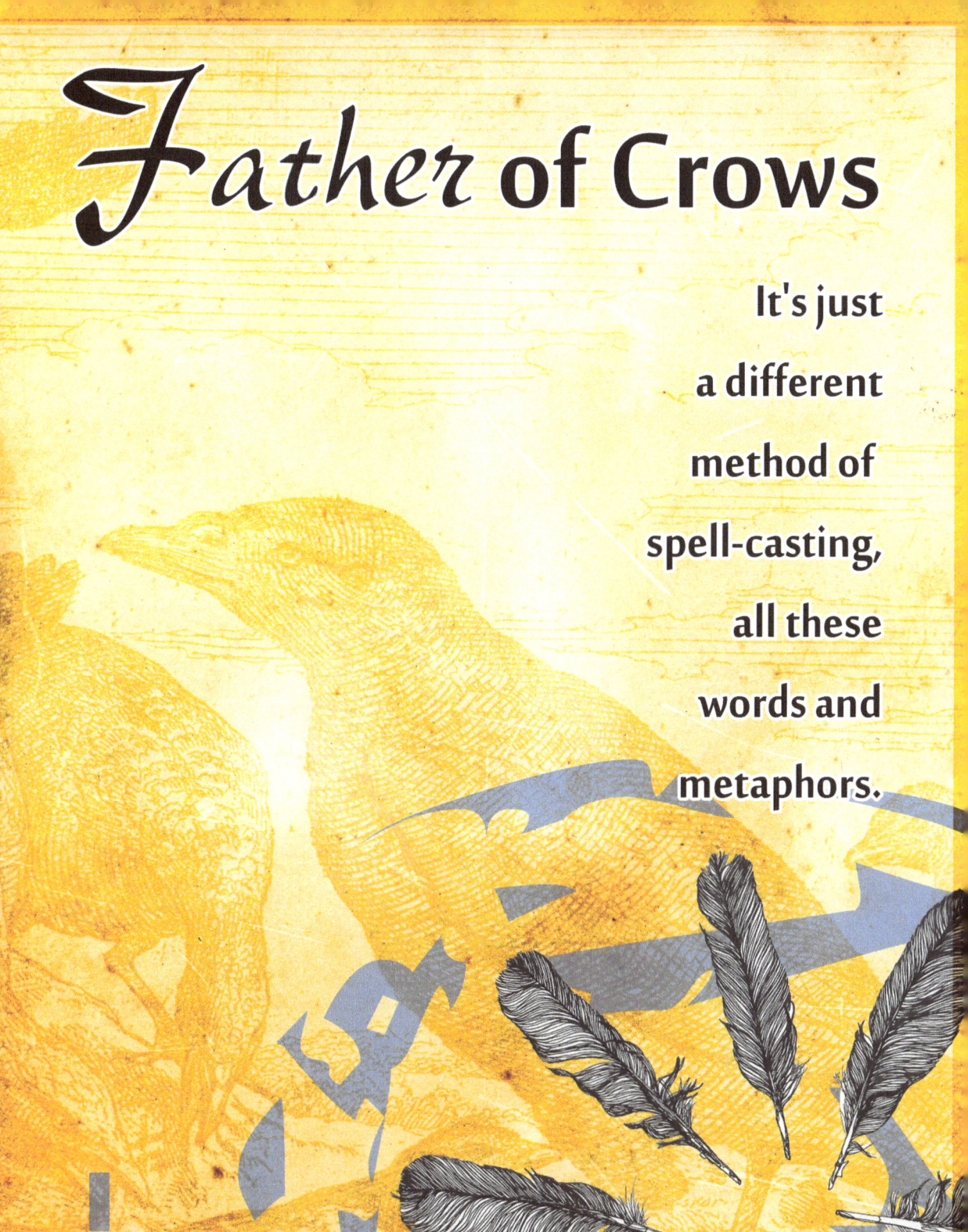

Father of Crows

It's just a different method of spell-casting, all these words and metaphors.

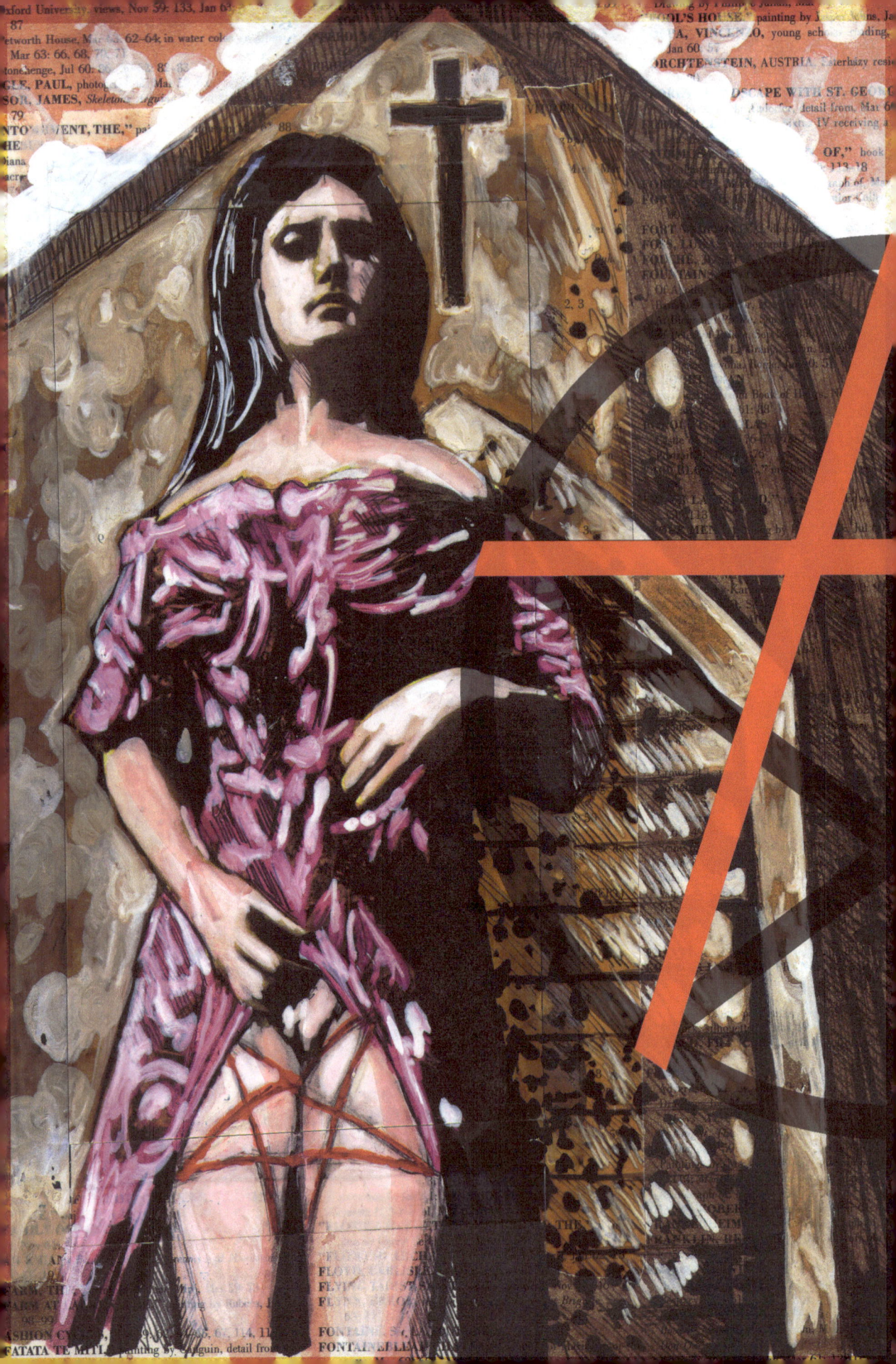

The Last Temptation of Hester Prynne

When your scarlet A
has a few extra
lines and angles...

Wear it proudly, girls.
Wear it proudly.

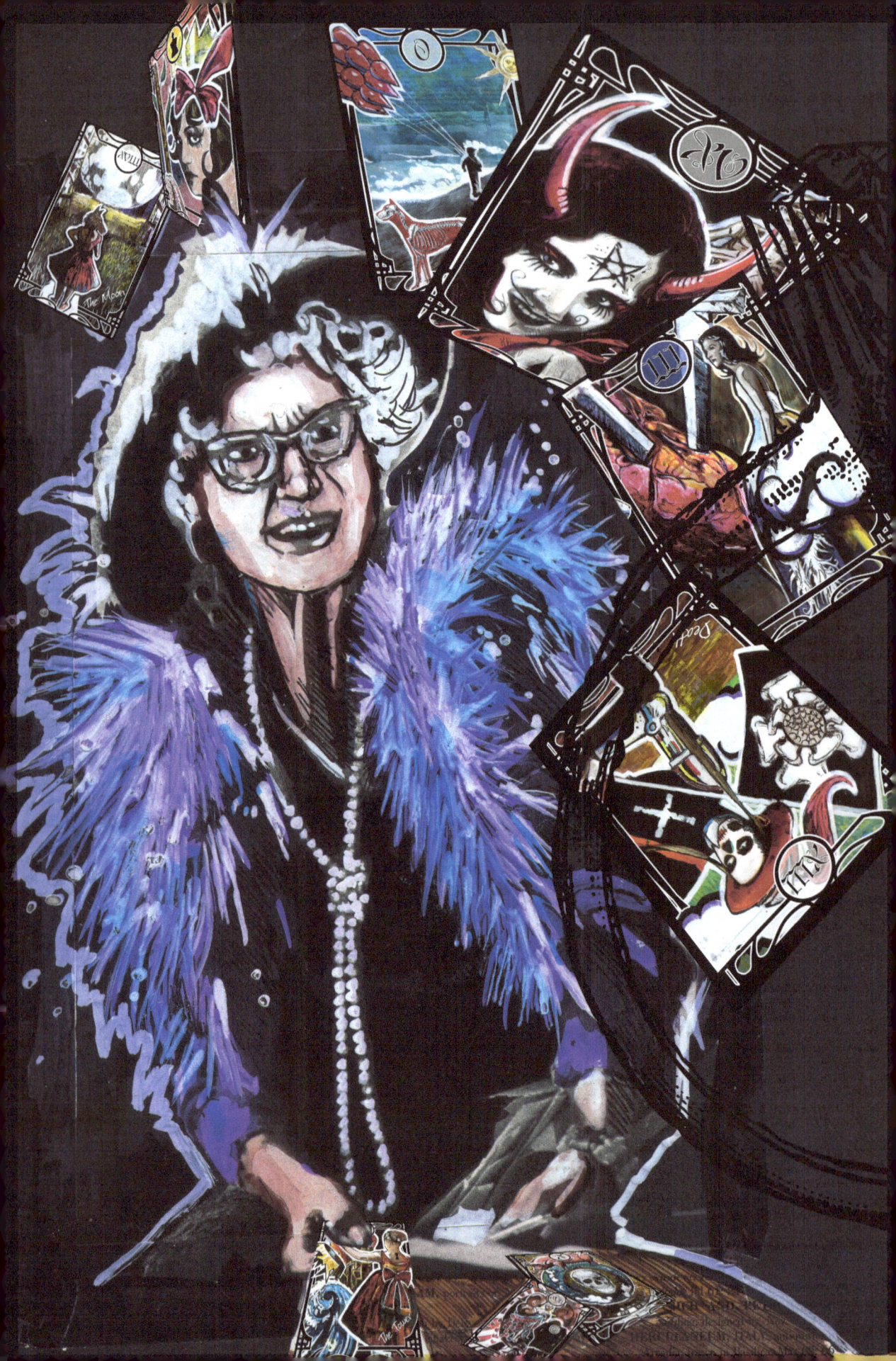

The Resplendent Queen of Diamonds

"If I am a fraud, my darlings,
if my cards were blank,
and prophecies empty,
maybe I was to be the blank space you
needed to clear your mind and see
your truth. Maybe I was a Buddhist-like
analogy reminding you that there are no
real answers. Maybe I am to be
the reflection for when you cannot
face yourself in the mirror.

Tabula Rasa for the late-in-life, if you will.

And like the diamonds absent
from my cards but present on
my fingers, my only real value is determined by the
owner. Or perhaps by the poor creature
who bled and died to unearth me, but that,
my darlings, is supply and demand.

Charlatans don't thrive where they aren't
needed, and there is quite a lovely bit of magic in that."

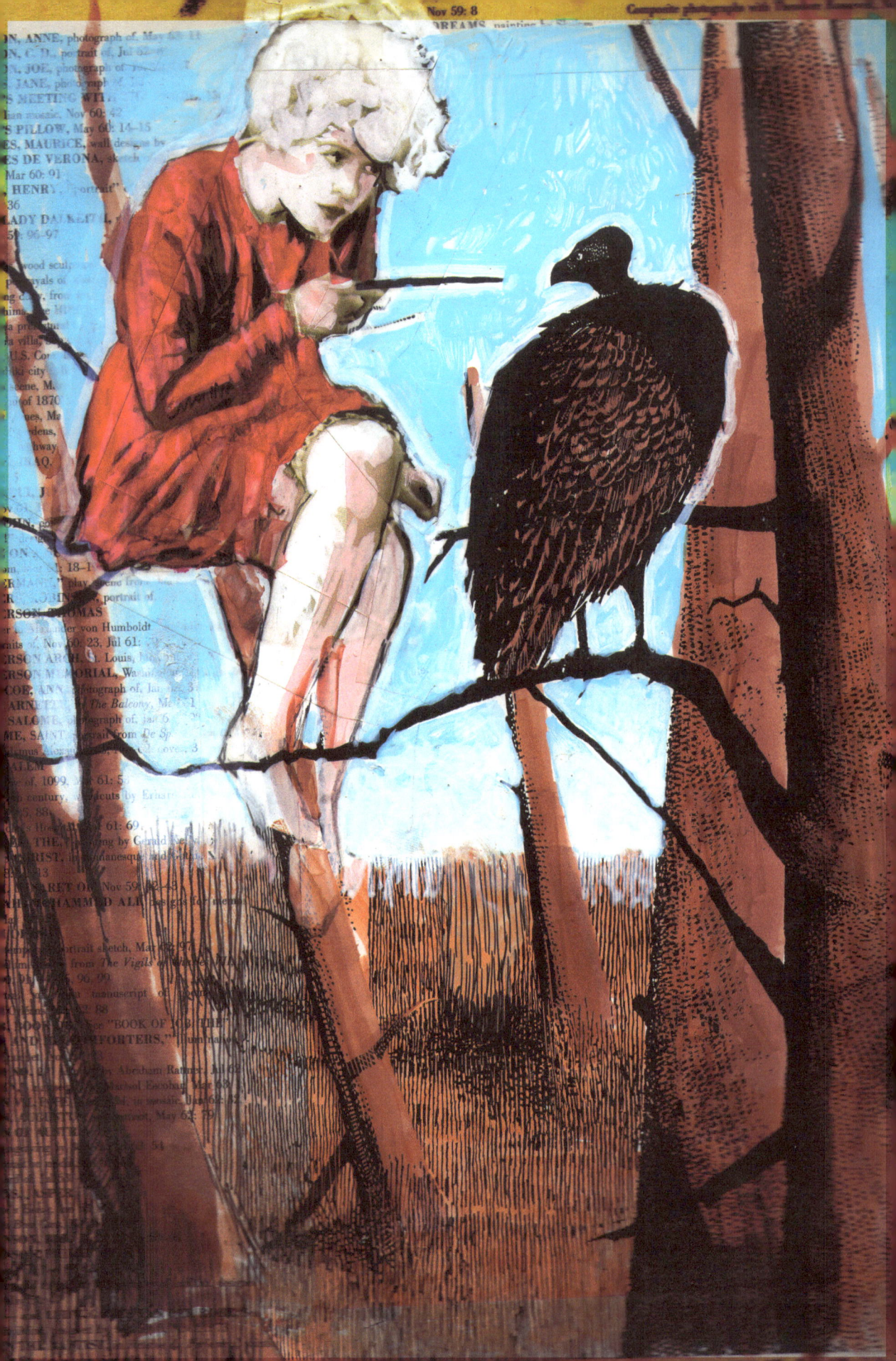

Ms Carrion's Classroom

The goal
was
to teach them
to start circling
before the final breath.

I would need warnings
throughout my life
and if I
couldn't
see them
in front of my face,
maybe
I'd remember
to
look to the sky.

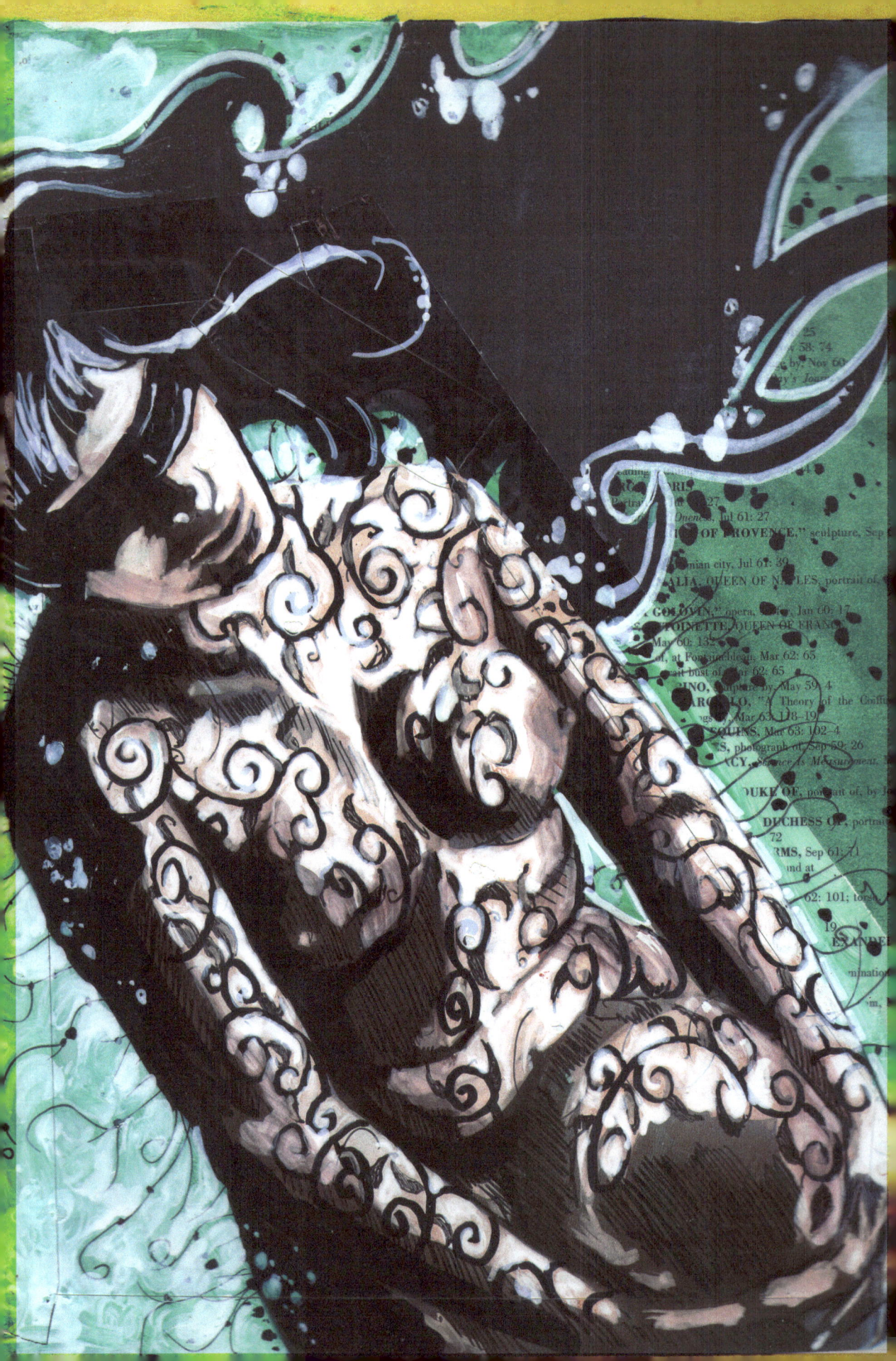

The Green Queen of Thorns.

Like stags during a rut, our thorns
interlocked years ago and we
remained entangled until death.

There was a lot of time to talk.

There was even more time to be silent.

But the scars we etched told lovely stories
and the howls of pain became our songs,
and all in all, there were far worse
ways to spend a lifetime.

Some people never got close
enough to become ensnared.

And some people chose to shed
their skins just to get away.

Everyone suffered, to be sure,
but we never suffered alone.

Illustrations by Steven Archer

Steven Archer is a painter, illustrator, sculptor, and mixed media artist, and a graduate of The Corcoran School of Art in Washington DC. He is the illustrator and author of a children's book *Luna Maris* (Imaginary Books).

Additionally, he is the co-founder, programmer, co-writer, and guitarist for the dark electronic-rock band Ego Likeness. As a solo artist, he is the face behind tribal-industrial act Stoneburner, the experimental project Hopeful Machines, and synthwave outfit QueenNeon.

Words by Donna Lynch

Donna Lynch is a horror author, poet, and spoken word artist. She is the author of two novels: *Isabel Burning* and *Red Horses* (Raw Dog Screaming Press) and the novella *Driving Through the Desert* (Thunderstorm Books/ RDSP), as well as several poetry collections and illustrated collaborations.

She is the co-founder, co-writer, lyricist, and singer of Ego Likeness, as well as a contributing live member of Stoneburner.

Archer and Lynch live in Maryland.

Witches is a follow-up collaborative work to 2010's *Daughters of Lilith* (RDSP).

www.ingramcontent.com/pod-product-compliance
Lightning Source LLC
Chambersburg PA
CBHW051840210526
45473CB00005B/1957